W9-CQC-540

Dear Nelson—

for your Library

Sincerely,

Paul Kadish

LIVONIA

"Livonia's Enterprises"
by Joan H. Kmenta

Produced in cooperation with the
Livonia Chamber of Commerce

Windsor Publications, Inc.
Chatsworth, California

LIVONIA

A Rich Past, A Golden Future

A Contemporary Portrait
By Tom Henderson

Windsor Publications, Inc.—Book Division
Managing Editor: Karen Story
Design Director: Alexander D'Anca
Photo Director: Susan L. Wells
Executive Editor: Pamela Schroeder

Staff for *Livonia: A Rich Past, A Golden Future*
Senior Manuscript Editor: Jerry Mosher
Photo Editor: Patty Salkeld
Editor, Corporate Profiles: Melissa Wells
Production Editor, Corporate Profiles: Justin Scupine
Customer Service Manager: Phyllis Feldman-
    Schroeder
Editorial Assistants: Elizabeth Anderson, Dominique
    Jones, Kim Kievman, Michael Nugwynne, Kathy
    B. Peyser, Theresa J. Solis
Publisher's Representatives, Corporate Profiles:
    Jennifer Olevitch, Kelly Lance
Layout Artist, Corporate Profiles: Sue Hartman
Layout Artist, Editorial: Bonnie Felt
Designer: Ellen Ifrah

Windsor Publications, Inc.
Elliot Martin, Chairman of the Board
James L. Fish III, Chief Operating Officer
Michele Sylvestro, Vice President/Sales-Marketing
Mac Buhler, Vice President/Acquisitions

©1990 Windsor Publications, Inc.
All rights reserved
Published 1990
Printed in the United States of America
First Edition

Library of Congress Cataloging-in-Publication Data
Henderson, Tom, 1948-
Livonia : a rich past, a golden future : a contempo-
rary portrait / by Tom Henderson. — 1st ed.
128 pp. 23 x 31 cm.
"Livonia's enterprises by Joan H. Kmenta." "Pub-
lished in cooperation with the Livonia Chamber of
Commerce."
Includes bibliographical references and index.
ISBN 0-89781-358-8
    1. Livonia (Mich.)—Civilization. 2. Livonia
(Mich.)—Description—Views. 3. Livonia (Mich.)—
Economic conditions. 4. Livonia (Mich.)—Industries.
I. Kmenta, Joan H. Livonia's enterprises. 1990. II.
Title.
    F574.L76H46 1990
977.4'33—dc 20   90-44741
                                             CIP

RIGHT: Carnival music, colorful lights, and delighted screams fill the night air during the weeklong Spree festival. The Michigan Stock Shop/Steve Fecht

CONTENTS

INTRODUCTION

Livonia's past is a microcosm of American history. "Go west," said Horace Greeley, but long before he said it, other adventurous and ambitious men and women had left the cities of the east for a life of unlimited promise and nearly as much hard work, carving homesteads and then small towns and villages out of the rugged wilderness.

On November 7, 1818, Dennison Palmer bought the first parcel of land in what was to become Livonia. Just 17 years later, the Indian tribes—the Ottawas, Potawatomis, Menominees, and Chippewas—had sold all their land in the area and headed west themselves, making way for the continued influx of farmers.

Roads were carved out in the meticulous, planned-out way of the white man—in a north-and-south grid system of parallel roads spaced one mile apart. Never mind that the roads often existed only on plat maps, or during dry, warm months when horses, mules, and oxen could pull a wagon over the planks or through the holes and ruts. Never mind that no one, then, really needed that many roads. Given the unflagging confidence of the time, it was clear that someday roads would be needed.

If there is one thread that weaves itself through the history of Livonia, it is planning—from the federal Land Ordinance of 1785, which bequeathed one square mile in each 36-square-mile township of the Northwest Territory for the sole benefit of public education, to the uproarious meeting in the loft of a bar in the mid-1960s, when politicians, city planners, and state highway officials made decisions about

freeways that would change the city forever and move it into the twenty-first century faster than anyone could have known.

"This is the best-planned city in America," says Ron Mardiros, Livonia's longtime city assessor. He may be forgiven for hyperbole, but, then, maybe he doesn't have

The Livonia Public Schools are a model for area districts. The Stevenson High School marching band stays on key while stepping out at a Memorial Day celebration. The Michigan Stock Shop/ Steve Fecht

to be forgiven. Maybe, just maybe, he is right. Livonia's six-mile-long industrial zone along the Jeffries Freeway, which bisects the city from east to west, was one of the first of its kind in the country. It is certainly the best-planned, largest continuous industrial zone in Michigan and a model for other Michigan cities, whose own politi-

cians wondered what in the world Livonia was doing when it was zoning so much land for industry. After all, everyone knew that suburban cities were bedroom communities, that industry and commerce were provinces of central cities like Detroit.

America in the 1950s was Ralph and Alice Kramden or Lucy and Ricky Ricardo

living in cramped big-city apartments. Late in the decade, when Lucy and Ricky moved to the suburbs, Ricky still commuted into the big city to work. It was the same in the 1960s, when Laura Petrie tended house in New Rochelle, but her husband, Rob, had to take the train into New York for employment. But Livonia ignored the media images and the conventional wisdom of the day. It refused to be a bedroom community, a mere adjunct to the real city nearby. It became a city of its own.

Today, Livonia doesn't have the problem of other suburban communities that have a hodge-podge of industry and commerce tucked into odd parcels of land, surrounded by residential neighbors who don't want them there. Livonia's industry is more or less tucked out of sight, with ready access to a network of freeways and railroads.

Nor does Livonia, a city of about 104,000, have the problem of gridlock, which faces other suburban Michigan communities that grew faster than the road infrastructure. In November 1989, Livonia voters approved the third in a series of 10-year bond proposals, a pay-as-you-go system that raises money before it will be spent for major road repairs and improvements. As roads need widening, they are widened, a simple-seeming policy that has served Livonia extremely well.

In nearby Oakland County to the north, gridlock brings traffic nearly to a halt every morning and evening, and planners wonder in despair where they will get the billions of dollars needed to build roads to service the people and industry that have been there for years. In Macomb County to the east, where serious development is just beginning, roads are already inadequate.

As other communities struggle with inadequate water pressure, too-narrow roads, and a lack of master planning for commercial and industrial zoning—in fact, some are ill-equipped to face the needs of 1990, much less the year 2000—Livonia is ready for the twenty-first century.

In many ways, southeastern Michigan has been the laboratory where the suburban city of the future—in Livonia's case, the present—was created. The world's first freeway—the Detroit Industrial Highway, which later became part of I-94, linking Detroit to Chicago—was built at the beginning of World War II to get workers to factories faster, so they could build more bombs and planes and speed up the pace of the "Arsenal of Democracy." And it was in Detroit that the first urban freeway was opened in 1942—it was called the Davison Limited Highway and was open and in use before anyone thought about what to do with cars that broke down. (It was built with curbs and without shoulders.) The rest of the country began to catch up in 1956, when the Federal Highway Act, which called for the construction of 41,000 miles of highways across the country, became the most ambitious highway plan since the Romans built the Appian Way.

And it was in southeastern Michigan, in nearby Southfield, that the first suburban shopping center in the nation was built— Northland, in 1954. And nothing has changed the face of metropolitan life more than freeways and shopping centers.

As the freeways were being built, no one envisioned the modern, self-contained suburban city. The Ricardo and Petrie scenario held sway. No one knew just how dramatic, how revolutionary, the changes would be.

When Livonia was incorporated in 1950, no one could have seen what it would look like in 1990. No one could have seen that what was then a farming community on the west end and a bedroom community on the east would become the prototypical city of the next century.

Yet, that is what it has become. It is a city that works. Its public school system is excellent, and Schoolcraft College was one of the first and remains one of the best-run community colleges in the state. Its recreational facilities are unmatched. Its

police force is a model for surrounding communities and even provides dispatch service for neighboring Redford Township. Yet the city's operating tax is the lowest in metropolitan Detroit and among the lowest in Michigan. Consider: Livonia added to its 1989 state equalized valuation (a figure that equals half the true property and building value) by $337 million, an increase of 16.5 percent in just a year and fully 25 percent of the growth for all of Wayne County. The value of property in the city climbed to $4.7 billion, more than 20 percent of the county total. Because of the industrial and commercial tax base, residents of the Livonia Public Schools paid lower property taxes in 1989 than residents of nearby Highland Park, Detroit, Westland, Garden City, and Northville.

With people, the saying is that life begins at 40, though the reality is that middle age is fast approaching. For Livonia, incorporated in 1950, its 40th anniversary begins the transition to adulthood. Its last undeveloped land to the north and west won't be undeveloped for long. For example, as recently as 1970, 24 percent of the city's land was undeveloped. By 1975, it had dropped to 22 percent and was less than 16 percent by 1980. By 1989, the year that marked the end of Livonia's adolescence, merely 8 percent was vacant land.

Much of that has occurred in the Golden Corridor along I-275, where hundreds of acres of woods and pastures are being converted to high-tech commercial development. Nearby, fields along Seven Mile Road or Newburgh have been cleared for large, upscale subdivisions. In this northwest corner past meets future, sometimes with a crash, more often with a melodic chime. Here, the twenty-first century has come early. Commercial and high-tech development that will fuel Livonia's future economy is being built, and graceful, spacious housing stock that will be Livonia's pride in future generations is taking shape on site plans and in those cleared fields.

FACING PAGE: The spiritual center of the city is the huge park complex across from City Hall, site of the week-long Spree celebration each June. The highlight comes on fireworks night, to the delight of thousands. Photo by Gary Quesada/ Korab Ltd.

1
A GOLDEN
FUTURE

Very few cities of 100,000
can boast of their own
symphony orchestra. The
Livonia Symphony Orches-
tra is one of the finest in
the Midwest. The Michigan
Stock Shop/Steve Fecht

WELCOME TO THE FUTURE

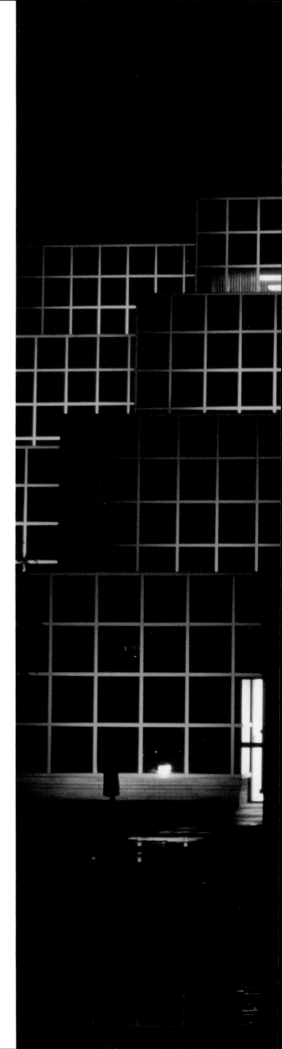

I f Horace Greeley were passing out advice in Livonia these days, he would tell young men and women: "Go northwest." It is in the northwest where most of the development action took place in the late 1980s, and where it will continue to take place through 2000 and beyond. As every businessperson knows, the three keys to business are location, location, location. In the northwest corner, you can find all three in abundance.

In the mid-1980s, it seemed as if zoning petitions and site plans for development projects along I-275 were coming before city council every month, each one seemingly grander than the one before. The bigger ones acquired single names—Jonna, Duke, Shenkman, and Victor. Linked together, they sounded like a powerful law firm; when completed, they would change the face of western Wayne County and finish the transition of Livonia from farmland to big city. Livonia's gangly adolescence was now full-fledged adulthood. There was brief but spirited opposition from some neighbors, opposition that withered with the quality-control measures instituted for the projects by the city council and by the developers themselves, who knew they had special terrain to work with and who were determined to develop something extra special, too.

Determined to develop something special—those five words sum up an attitude that has prevailed in Livonia since settlers first arrived. It's an attitude that arrived with

The geometric patterns of the Cambridge Office Center create an impressive design at night. Photo by Balthazar Korab

Livonia is about development, but it is also about nature preserves, forests, and parks. Deer, beaver, rabbits, and Canada geese flourish, and give a reminder of the bounty found here by early settlers who were lured by the cheap price of land. Photo by Balthazar Korab

Freeways are the arteries that carried the lifeblood of development and industry to Livonia. The industrial belt runs for six miles along the Jeffries Freeway, and the Golden Corridor of commercial development runs along I-275. The Michigan Stock Shop/Steve Fecht

Dennison Palmer in 1818, when he was the first white man to buy a parcel of land in the area, and it was an attitude that was expressed argumentatively in a historic meeting in the mid-1960s in a loft of a bar in Plymouth, a meeting that made all that development in the northwest corner possible. As we continue to look forward at development along the Golden Corridor, it's time to take a look backward, too.

A HISTORY LESSON

Palmer bought his land in 1818, and just 17 years later the Indians decided things were getting a bit too crowded, and so they sold the rest of their land and most of them headed west. By 1845, the last Potawatomi village—called Pojomaka and located at what is now Grand River and Eight Mile just north of present-day Livonia—was a

ghost town, its last residents finally following their brethren in the search for peace and quiet.

The white man so quickly replacing the Indian would have come as a shock to Edward Tiffin, a former U.S. surveyor general. In 1780, he announced that southeastern Michigan was "swampy, sandy and unfit for agriculture and habitation." It wasn't, he said, even worth surveying.

The U.S. victory in the War of 1812 opened up the Northwest Territory, of which Michigan was a part. Immigrants began trickling in. The trickle became a stream and then a river with the opening of the Erie Canal in 1825.

Settlers would pile their belongings on a barge or a boat, ride the Erie into the Great Lakes, and then head west. Many of them landed in Detroit and stayed there. The more adventuresome and industrious continued west, first storing their belongings in Detroit, then following the Rouge River inland from the Detroit River, usually on foot, and occasionally on horseback. They'd head west along the Rouge, following whatever creek or tributary looked promising, and stop when they found suitable land.

Land was going for $1.25 to $2 an acre, and for that kind of money, you didn't just stop at the first piece of dry land you found. You looked for a bit of paradise. Some found it in Dearborn, others kept going to what is now Livonia or, even farther, to Plymouth.

Much of the buying and selling of land was speculative. Eighty acres that sold for $100 in 1828 would be sold two years later for $300 and again the next year for $400. There were few actual farms in the Livonia area and no town to speak of.

Bucklin Township—named for William Bucklin, an early justice of the peace—was organized as a governmental unit in 1827 and eventually became four full townships, including Livonia. On May 28 of that year, the first township meeting was held and the princely sum of $100 was raised to run the township for a year. In some ways, concerns haven't changed: at the first meeting an ordinance was enacted to limit the height of fences to four and a half feet.

In 1829, Bucklin was divided into Nankin on the west and Pekin on the east. Why those names? Missionary activity in China was all the rage then, the Orient having captured the imagination of the popular press, and locals thought it would be nice to name their townships after two cities in China.

In 1834, another township was carved out. It was called Livonia, after a city in New York from which many of the settlers had come. (The New York town, in turn, had been named after a powerful and prosperous nation in Eastern Europe, later to be conquered and divided between Latvia and Estonia and even later to be swallowed up by the Soviet Union.)

In 1838 came that which would lead to all the rest—the first road from Detroit. It was a plank road, named for the boards that were laid across its many ruts and holes. It was a private road, named Plymouth Road, and the fare was a penny a mile, considered steep in that day.

Rivers have always led to development—first rivers of water and, later, rivers of concrete or asphalt. Even in 1838, optimistic planners called the roads "highways," though they were often impassable. But with a population of just 1,169 in 1840 and only 1,460 as recently as 1900, Livonia didn't need much in the way of roads—it was still primarily farmland.

The post-World War II exodus to the suburbs changed all that. In 1940, Livonia had grown to just 8,728. By 1960, 10 years after its incorporation as a city, the population was 66,702, and it was obvious that the old, two-lane surface streets would no longer suffice.

Industry once followed rivers or train lines; now it followed highways and freeways. U.S. 10 led to Southfield, home of

RIGHT: With its well-planned network of highways, Livonia is at the hub of popular destinations in southeast Michigan, such as airports, universities, sporting events, and cultural attractions. The Michigan Stock Shop/Steve Fecht

BELOW: Upon its completion, workers, neighbors, and architectural critics all praised the breathtaking CBS/Fox Video headquarters, constructed just off I-275. Photo by Beth Singer

the nation's first suburban shopping center. I-75 resulted in the office boom in Troy. The Jeffries brought business west to Livonia. I-275, opened in 1977, was christened the "Golden Corridor" long before much development or any gold was found in the rolling hills along the freeway.

But where rivers were built by nature and got where they were by process of earthquake, glacier movement, and gravity, freeways appeared by more artificial means. People decided where they would go, and consequently, where the industry and commerce would go, too. Such decisions made some cities rich and some men millionaires. Land at a freeway exit was much more valuable than land without an exit. Cities along the freeway, like Livonia, were much more likely to prosper than cities that were merely nearby, like Garden City.

And so one of the most important meetings in the history of Livonia or western Wayne County took place one night in the mid-1960s in an attempt to decide where to put in exits along the proposed east-west Jeffries Freeway, and where to put in the north-south I-275 freeway at the west end of the county.

PREVIOUS PAGE:
Whether it's ultramodern
commercial developments
along I-275, or upscale
housing projects nearby,
construction remains an
integral component of Livonia's present and future.
Photo by Balthazar Korab

Harvey Moelke was then mayor of Livonia, an honest but stubborn man, say friends and foes. Contentious, stubborn, and argumentative, he was famous for his fights with city council and for vetoing much of what it tried to do.

Moelke wanted the Jeffries to run north of its present route, and he wanted I-275 to come in along Livonia's western border, along Haggerty Road and right along the brand new Schoolcraft College.

There was one thing wrong with his plan for I-275—only the land to the east of the freeway would be in Livonia. The western edge would be in Plymouth Township. The movers and shakers in Livonia knew that eventually the freeway would bring commerce and development to those fields and forests, and they wanted all of that to benefit Livonia's tax base. The freeway would have to be moved east; there was no doubt about it.

Which is where the all-night meeting in the loft of the Round Table in Plymouth came in. There were no Sunshine laws in those days; no reporters were invited and no minutes were kept. Angelo DiPonio, a powerful and influential developer who owned much of the land in the area, organized the meeting. State highway department bosses and all seven city council members came, but Moelke wasn't invited.

The meeting began at 5 p.m. and ended at 4 a.m. By the end of the night, there was a consensus. The Jeffries would go where it is now (which resulted in the six-mile industrial zone that ran along it), and I-275 would bend into Livonia south of Eight Mile. (Without that bend, the land along the freeway today would just be other parcels of land instead of some of the most valuable real estate in Michigan.) Though it seems incomprehensible now, state officials wanted the Jeffries to be built as a

rural freeway, that is, at surface level. Far-sighted council members held out for, and won, permission to have the freeway built as an urban freeway, recessed into the ground. Livonia also got more exit and entrance ramps than the state originally wanted, which also facilitated industrial development nearby.

Councilmember Edward McNamara, later perhaps the best mayor in Livonia history and today Wayne County's chief executive, attended the meeting and then presented Moelke with the results. Moelke, contentious as he was, was also a realist; he had no choice but to go along.

Two decades later, after fits and starts, development finally began along I-275. Though it was dubbed the "Golden Corridor" shortly after it opened, McNamara admits: "None of us visualized how valuable that land would ultimately become." Ironically, McNamara owns land at Five Mile just west of I-275. The land would be much more valuable than it is except that there isn't an exit ramp at Five Mile. Which was a lesson to McNamara and the end of the history lesson.

NORTHWEST LIVONIA: A LESSON IN PLANNING

There has been some criticism of the scope of development in northwest Livonia from developers in nearby cities, whose buildings often were half empty and who feared a glut in the market. It wasn't a fear shared by James Jonna, president and CEO of the Jonna Companies, which consisted of a construction company, a holding company, and a leasing and marketing company.

What was unofficially known as the Jonna Project is officially called Chestnut Hills, 42 acres of land west of I-275 and adjacent to Haggerty Road, south of Eight Mile Road. Plans included a hotel, two office buildings, a parking deck, and three restaurants.

Jonna didn't care that there was a glut

of space in Oakland County to the north. And he wasn't concerned with other projects creating a glut along the Golden Corridor of I-275. Why? Location, location, location—he had it and no one was going to take it away from him. "By the time we come on line, the surplus in Livonia will be gone," he said in 1989 as he neared the end of a long struggle with the state's Department of Natural Resources over how to protect the wetlands on his property. "I-275 will continue to grow. That's guaranteed. My friends say, 'Jimmy, aren't you worried?' And I say, 'No way.'"

Why was he so confident? He ticked off a series of numbers and letters. "M-14, M-23, I-94, I-275, I-96." Those are codes of sort for location, location, etc. M-14 heads west to Ann Arbor, the University of Michigan, and a pocket of university-related research, development, and high-tech. M-23 nearby links Toledo to the south with Flint to the north. I-94 joins Detroit to Chicago, and accesses two major airports: Metro Airport, a regional hub for Northwest Airlines (whose regional data, computer, and reservation center recently opened in Livonia); and Willow Run. I-275 is the Golden Corridor that links I-94 with I-96. And I-96 joins Detroit to Lansing, the state capital, and Michigan State University, the state's largest university and another research and high-tech center. With a major highway network like that, Jonna knew glut wasn't a four-letter word, it was a four-letter impossibility.

William Roskelly knows what gluts aren't. When you put up a sign announcing a future housing project and your phone rings off the hook, that's not a glut. Roskelly is a principal in the Shenkman project, an elegantly planned collection of offices, condominiums, and houses on 170 acres of land east of I-275 along Newburgh Road, between Six and Seven Mile roads. It is currently in the preliminary stages. Soon after putting up two small signs announcing the project, he had 300

names on a waiting list, extraordinary considering there would be just 366 condominiums or houses in all. "There may be a glut of space in southeastern Michigan, but it's not geographically desirable space," he says. Left unsaid was the corollary: Livonia is desirable, geographically and otherwise.

Both east and west of I-275 are a well-planned series of subdivisions—some already built, some on the drawing boards—that will house Livonians in style through the next century. Quakertown was built in the early 1980s, north of Five Mile and west of I-275, where some lucky owners of single-family homes have creeks winding through their backyards. Laurel Woods and The Woods, two established condominium projects, sit nestled amongst towering shade trees. At the new Greenfield Villas condominiums just to their east, small, freshly planted trees don't give much shade, yet, but they will. Farther to the east, north of Seven Mile and east of Newburgh, there are new and

expansive housing projects such as Willow Woods, Whispering Hills, and Fox Creek Meadows. And there's Laurel Park South and Livonia Hills Estates.

Throughout the area, housing blends in harmoniously with existing or planned commercial development. Both will serve Livonia well long after current residents are gone.

Harmony. It's another thread that weaves itself through Livonia's history. Duke Associates' office project, known officially as The Seven Mile Crossing, is an example. It was built and opened in 1987 on land along I-275 owned by Schoolcraft College. The development was good for tax purposes because it returned land to the tax rolls. And it was and will be a boon for the college; under terms of the lease, the buildings in the project will revert to ownership of the school in 2062. Two buildings are completed on the site, totalling 260,000 square feet, and a third, of 130,000 feet, is in the planning stages. And they are so attractive that the Detroit Chamber of Commerce used one of them on the cover of its annual publication in 1989.

Though James Jonna of the Jonna project and Ernest Maddock of Duke might disagree, city fathers consider the jewel of the I-275 corridor to be Victor Corporate Park, 105 acres on the east side of the freeway north of Seven Mile Road.

Progress along the freeway had been plodding along in fits and starts, when in 1985 a young developer named David Johnson, a 1967 graduate of Livonia's Bentley High School, told city officials he had acquired land along the freeway and wanted to build a grandiose corporate park

filled with Fortune 500 companies and incorporating the finest in workmanship and materials.

Victor—named for Johnson's father, a Swedish immigrant—would evolve in a manner mirroring that of the corridor as a whole, in fits and starts. Zoning approval was quick, despite some protest by neighbors who had grown accustomed to living next to a forest. But actual development was anything but quick.

Finally, in April 1988 Johnson landed his first Fortune 500 company. Digital Corporation announced it had bought some of Johnson's land at the north end of the project and would consolidate five offices it leased in nearby communities into a 350,000-square-foot building it would own. (A slowdown in its business worldwide has delayed the project, but Digital officials say they remain committed to the site and a regional headquarters.)

In July 1988, site-plan approval was given to the first building in the project, a five-story, $22-million, 240-room Embassy Suites Hotel that opened in December 1989. And what a hotel it was! Each guest suite included a living room, bedroom, wet bar, refrigerator, microwave, two telephones, and two televisions. And all guests were served a complimentary, cooked-to-order breakfast in the morning, and a two-hour complimentary cocktail party was held in the evening.

But the major breakthrough at Victor occurred in September 1988 when, after months of negotiations, Johnson, a man of

vision but not enough money, secured a much-needed partner. Hillman Properties Inc., a Pittsburgh-based firm that is one of the largest privately owned industrial companies in the world, has a track record of building some of the finest complexes in the U.S.

Other Hillman ventures included the Xerox Center in Chicago; International Place in Boston; Tower Bridge in Philadelphia; Fifth Avenue Place in Pittsburgh; Stadium Towers in Anaheim, California; and Yerba Buena West in San Francisco.

"They have very, very, very deep pockets," said a relieved Johnson. "Where somebody else needs to compromise on a building, we can bring the best product to the market."

Ground was broken in October 1989 on Hillman's first building, a five-story, 115,000-square-foot office building featuring classic design, red brick, cast stone, granite, and tinted glass. Traditional yet

LEFT: Just one of the outstanding architectural structures at the Laurel Park Place complex is the Laurel Park Place office building, developed under the guidance of Schostak Brothers developers. Photo by Gary Quesada/Korab Ltd.

FACING PAGE, TOP: Laurel Park Place—from its marble floors, to arched entryways, to stores that are anything but ordinary— is a showcase of fine shopping. Photo by Gary Quesada/Korab Ltd.

FACING PAGE, BOTTOM: Seven Mile Crossing, an office project by Duke Associates, is an innovative marriage between the private sector and the public sector. Schoolcraft Community College leases the land to Duke and will eventually own the series of three office buildings constructed by Duke. Michigan Stock Shop/Steve Fecht

modern, the building includes shower and locker facilities for men and women wishing to take advantage of the jogging track that runs throughout the complex. And another Hillman building is planned for a site across from a nearby, reflecting pond. Plans call for the park to be completed in 1999 and to include two million square feet of office space in nine buildings, ranging from 4 to 12 stories.

Any talk of jewels would be remiss without mentioning another jewel—the Laurel Park Place complex at Newburgh Road and Six Mile, just east of I-275.

It, too, mirrored the on-again-off-again development of the corridor. Zoning was in place for more than a decade before the upscale Jacobson's department store finally opened in the summer of 1987. Other development on the site was quick to materialize under the guidance of Schostak Brothers developers.

Both a Marriott mid-rise hotel and a Marriott Courtyard hotel opened in 1989. Also built were the three-building Laurel Office Park, the Powercourt office building, and, most impressive of all, the Laurel Park Place mall.

Somehow the word "mall" is inadequate when describing the series of shops adjacent to Jacobson's. Opened late in 1989 in time for the shopping season, the mall features upscale shops. Entry to the mall is through a series of tall, elegant arches. Inside, customers walk on beautiful marble agglomerate, which is made of marble dust and chips set in epoxy and polished to a sheen.

THE INDUSTRIAL CORRIDOR

While the city's northwest corner was where much of the development that would continue Livonia on its course for the next century was occurring, there was still plenty going on in the older, industrial corridor to the south. There, operations ranged from small job shops supplying parts to the auto industry to huge opera-

tions such as the headquarters for Awrey Bakery.

Changes in the way the automakers conducted their business in the late 1980s contributed a sense of energy and technology throughout the area.

The *London Economist* called it Automation Alley and said it is the hot spot in the world of high-tech engineering and design. The hot spot, said the publication, is no longer Silicon Valley in California, nor is it Route 128 in Boston. Rather, it is a loosely defined region in southeastern Michigan whose epicenter is Livonia and its industrial corridor.

Automation Alley is an outgrowth of the revitalization of the American auto industry, which responded vigorously, if slowly at first, to competition from Japan and Europe.

Several things were part of that revitalization. Just-in-time delivery required suppliers to be closer to manufacturing centers. Statistical Process Control, a method of quality control that could prove which suppliers made the best parts, required investments for technology and training. And, most important, the Big Three decided it no longer made sense to engineer all the parts that went into their cars; they required suppliers to do the engineering. If Ford or Chrysler no longer builds something in-house, it no longer engineers it in-house. That required suppliers to expand their research and development operations and has been a boon for Livonia.

Borg-Warner, for example, spent $6 million in 1988 to house its research and development team in a 60,000-square-foot facility in the Livonia Tech Center, a new complex tucked unobtrusively into the woods north of Plymouth Road and west of Middlebelt, along the southern end of the industrial corridor. Borg-Warner plans to expand there to 200,000 square feet.

In that same Tech Center is the research and development arm of a new joint-venture company that has excited city officials unlike few others. It is ARCAD, Inc., and is literally a new auto firm that plans on becoming a worldwide giant. ARCAD is both an acronym for Association of Renault and Chrysler for Automotive Development and a play on the industry term CAD, which stands for computer-aided design. The new company will operate manufacturing plants in the U.S. and Europe to produce low-end utility and recreational vehicles for worldwide distribution.

ARCAD came into being on paper in June 1989 and by the end of August its employees were at work in the Tech Center. Operations were so brisk that employment climbed from 150 to 200 by the end of the year, and its brand new 69,000-square-foot building was expanded to 100,000 square feet.

Excitement in the industrial corridor isn't confined to huge operations with 200 employees in buildings of 100,000 square feet. There's just as much excitement in a small, easy-to-miss, six-person office on Industrial Drive.

The office houses the U.S. operations of FATA Automation. Years from now, when historians assess the success or failure of *glasnost* and *perestroika* in the Soviet Union, a footnote may very well be reserved for FATA and its Livonia manager, Anna Migliulo.

Restructuring the bureaucratic maze of Soviet society is a grand and daring scheme involving world leaders and incredible changes in philosophy. But whether it succeeds or not depends less on political maneuvering and more on such mundane things as having enough bread on the table and enough refrigeration units to keep the crops from rotting at distribution centers.

And that's where FATA comes in. FATA European Group is a worldwide, Italian-based company whose ties to Russia go back to 1959, when it built its first factory in

Siberia. Since then, it has built several turn-key factories in the Soviet Union for food processing and producing cardboard boxes and other food packaging. (Turn-key operations are those in which the contractor builds the entire plant, then turns the keys over to the owner.)

In 1987 FATA became the first Western firm to establish a joint-venture agreement with the Soviet Union, with 27 percent interest in a plant that had a target of building 250,000 refrigeration units in its first year of operation in 1990.

"That's an absurd total by Western standards, but by Soviet standards, it's just right," says Migliulo, the daughter of the former Italian ambassador to Moscow and herself a former mathematics major at Moscow State University. (She received her master's degree in public and private management from Yale.)

Migliulo speaks fluent Russian and English and opened up the Livonia office in 1988 to serve as U.S. headquarters for FATA's attempt to find joint-venture American partners for future Soviet operations. "Our research showed us there were fantastic opportunities in the U.S.," says Migliulo, noting that both the U.S. and Russia share similar economies of scale.

Research also showed her that Livonia, of all the places in the U.S., was the place to pursue those fantastic opportunities.

GREAT LIVONIA PEOPLE

Acity is more than the sum of its industrial belts, commercial zones, hotel complexes, and shopping centers, of course. Those things will tell you about the economic climate of a place, but it's the people who give you a feel for what a city is really all about.

Here are just a few of Livonia's interesting residents—from a college president who used to teach piano, to a volunteer who helped bring Greenmead Historical Village into existence, to a retarded man who tools around town on his bicycle bringing love to those he finds, especially his pals at the fire station, to a police chief who held on to his membership in the bricklayers' union for years just in case being a cop didn't work out, to a retiree who writes training manuals for inner-city poor trying to learn a trade.

SISTER MARY FRANCILENE

She used to teach the tune; now, as president of highly regarded Madonna College, she calls it. Sit in with Sister Mary Francilene as she conducts a planning session for a school fund-raiser and you'll quickly learn not to mistake that huge smile for softness. Behind it lurks a firmness and decisiveness that would do Lee Iacocca proud.

Smile? Sister Francilene's makes the Cheshire cat's look like a grimace. And energy? She crackles with electricity as she surges down hallways and into meetings.

Livonia's most precious resource is its people. Photo by Clifford Hausner/After-Image

Edison could tap into her and forget nuclear power.

But it's an energy as well controlled as power through a line. The Exxon Corporation recently named her one of the top college or university presidents in the country for the way she has managed the school, whose enrollment is at an all-time high at more than 4,100.

"She's effective and efficient," says Andrea Nodge, Madonna's director of public relations, who has watched Sister Francilene run many meetings. "When you're in a meeting with her, she's very open and will ask you your opinion, but when it's time to make a decision—boom, boom, boom—she makes it."

Sister Francilene's smile is the first thing that greets visitors. The second is a firm—make that FIRM—handshake. But if you plan on spending any time with her, don't plan on getting comfortable in her big office; you'll be up and off as she scurries from one place to another to conduct business on Madonna's grounds or in the community.

Sister Francilene is a conductor elsewhere, too—with the Livonia Symphony Orchestra as a regular guest conductor. "I always direct marches, in keeping with my personality," she jokes. Sister Francilene was a musician and a music teacher long before it was decided she would become Madonna's president. She still sings in the Felician Sisters Choir and has found time for such secular pursuits as serving on the board of directors of the Livonia Chamber of Commerce (she is in her second six-year term) and on the board of the Detroit Learning and Speech Center.

Sister Francilene was the first of six children born to Hector and Irene VandeVyver.

She and a younger sister entered the sisterhood. (Sister Joyce was principal of St. Sabrina School in nearby Dearborn Heights and was named in 1989 as the director of the newly opened child day-care program at St. Mary Hospital in Livonia.)

"I always wanted to join the sisterhood, even as a young girl in elementary school," explained Sister Francilene. "I feel fortunate I've always had a calling to this lifestyle. A very strong motivation in my life is the sense of commitment to the Lord."

Sister Francilene is 49 and looks 39. She was 34 and looked 24 when she became Madonna's president. Despite a tenderness in years and looks, she had no hesitation about assuming the presidency and has never looked back wistfully to her days as piano teacher at Livonia's Ladywood High School.

"I am a person who enjoys what they're doing. When I was a music teacher, I really enjoyed it, and I was good at it," she says. "When I have a new responsibility, I work at it very enthusiastically, 100 percent."

Francilene hadn't aspired to administration. She became a college president because she was asked by one of her superiors. As part of her vow of obedience, she accepted.

Under Sister Francilene, Madonna's budget has grown from about $2.7 million to more than $14 million, and the school has continued to expand its innovative programs. (In 1989, it won out over 12 other state schools in a competitive bidding process to offer a business degree program to employees of Michigan Bell.)

Madonna is the only college or university in the state with a full-support program for the deaf. The school began its adult education program well before it became a staple at other schools. (Half its enrollment is adult and the median age of all students is 29; barely half the enrollment at the school is Catholic, despite its name.) The school offered one of the first liberal arts majors in gerontology and has programs in hospice education and emergency medical technology. And its criminal justice program is one of the school's most popular and successful programs, with 210 students.

"We're building a sense of community here," says Sister Francilene. "This isn't just a job, bringing people together for a paycheck."

As the school has grown, so, too, has Sister Francilene. "I've developed a greater listening capacity. And because I have a fast metabolism—I speak fast and walk fast—I've had to slow down and give a presence of being with those who want to talk to me."

How else? "In my ability to write." And, with a chuckle, "my ability to answer reporters."

BRIAN LOWE

Brian Lowe is a familiar sight to Livonia residents as he tools around town on his bicycle. Gregarious and friendly, he'll stop and chat with pedestrians waiting at a streetlight, or pull onto the running track at Bentley High School to ride alongside the joggers. Usually, though, Lowe can be spotted at or near one of the city's fire stations.

Lowe, 39, wasn't always so loquacious. Mentally handicapped, Lowe rarely talked before he started showing up at fire stations in 1984. He'd look at the equipment, and as the firefighters began talking to their new friend more and more, he began talking back.

"These are his friends," says his mother, Irene, of the firefighters. "They encouraged his speech. They went beyond the line of duty."

Firefighting is frenetic activity and danger interspersed with time to kill. When Brian first started showing up on his bike, they could have turned a cold shoulder to him and pushed him away. But it was a lull time, and they began talking to him, taking him under their wing.

His mom says: "When Brian was 3½

years old, we were told he would never be able to talk or ride a bike. He is doing both, now, nonstop. He did have speech therapy, but the best therapy was administered by the firefighters of Livonia. They didn't do it with a siren or flashing red lights. They did it with their hearts. They tell him everything about the trucks and what goes on at the fire station. He showed us how to push on the chest to revive a person. It's all so exciting and important to him, he is forced to tell us all about it when he comes home."

For five years, Brian rode his bike around town. Finally, he could ride it no farther, the miles having taken their toll. And so, one day in the summer of 1989, the firefighters told him to come on down to Station No. 1. When he got there, they had a brand-new Schwinn Cruiser for him.

EDWARD MCNAMARA

Edward McNamara was Livonia's larger-than-life mayor for 16 years, before he became Wayne County's chief executive in 1987. City Hall reporters in Livonia missed him the most; he is a consummate politician who doesn't talk like one.

About his early days in politics, when he was elected a Democratic precinct delegate in Detroit in 1948 at the age of 22, McNamara says: "In those days, they [party regulars] used to go in a room and copy names out of the phone book on their petitions. I was stupid enough to go door to door." But that year, the petitions were challenged as phonies and only his held up.

By 1959, McNamara was on the school board in Dearborn, serving as a manager at Michigan Bell, and attending law school at the University of Detroit. He was making the grand total of $76 a week, "and I figured I was on my way. We decided I would resign from the school board, move

RIGHT: Exuding youth and energy, Sister Mary Francilene is the strong-willed president of Madonna College. The Exxon Corporation recently named her one of the top college or university presidents in the U.S. The Michigan Stock Shop/Steve Fecht

BELOW: Livonia's police chief, William Crayk, is equally suited to running the new police station or using his skill as a bricklayer to remodel his home. The Michigan Stock Shop/ Steve Fecht

FAR RIGHT: Brian Lowe, familiar man-about-town on his ever-present bicycle, shines up the new bike that was given to him by the Livonia Fire Department. The Michigan Stock Shop/ Steve Fecht

to Livonia and never get involved in politics again. I was clean for three years."

He won election to Livonia's city council in 1962 and was elected council president in 1968.

Harvey Moelke, a feisty politician with a well deserved reputation for being quarrel-

some, was the incumbent mayor when McNamara challenged him in 1970. "It was a hard-fought, bitter campaign," says McNamara, who had the rare backing of a united city council, which wasn't so much pro-McNamara as anti-Moelke.

They were locked in a tight, dead-even

campaign when McNamara pulled what he calls the dirtiest trick of his political career. His people took out an ad in the *Livonia Observer* with a picture of Moelke's house, which, says McNamara, looked much more expensive from the outside than it actually was. "The caption said, 'Moelke pays $800 in taxes. How much do you pay?'" laughed McNamara. "He was madder than hell. He announced he was going to have an open house so people could see the house wasn't fixed up on the inside. But his wife refused."

Moelke canceled the open house and lost the election.

When McNamara left for county government, even many of his friends and supporters thought he had finally bitten off more than he could chew. The county had become a joke in government circles; it was out of money, badly in debt, and operating a budget as if red ink were the only kind.

Moreover, he was a suburbanite taking over one of the largest urban counties in the country—it includes the entire city of Detroit—and he was a white man who would need to cut deals with wary black politicians. Any deals with the state government in Lansing for financial help would involve, everyone agreed, the miraculous consent of outstate politicians long since grown antagonistic to the problems of a county down in the southeast corner of Michigan, far, far away from their own constituents.

In December 1987, McNamara got the state-aid package just about everyone but he thought was wishful thinking at best. "I'll give him credit," says Republican staff member Bill Gnodtke. "Whether you like him or not, he gets up here and puts his hand on the wheel."

McNamara, not afraid to come with hat in hand, prowled the halls and lobbies of state government, cornering legislators, shaking hands, patting backs, twisting arms, and begging if begging was required.

"You know the rotunda area outside the chambers, where the lobbyists hang out. McNamara was in that space for weeks," says Representative Lyn Bankes, a Republican from Livonia. "He was still there at 12:20 in the morning. It was truly amazing."

The county, which many legislators had favored putting into receivership, was given financial aid. Today, it operates in the black and has trimmed deficits dramatically. No longer do Detroiters wonder if a

Ed McNamara, Livonia's longtime mayor, is now the chief executive for Wayne County, which includes Detroit. He is credited with getting the county's budget out of the red and into the black. The Michigan Stock Shop/Steve Fecht

suburbanite has their interests at heart. No one seems to notice anymore that McNamara is white.

That he's done so well isn't a surprise to his former secretary, Madeline Ryan, who turned down his pitch to move with him from Livonia City Hall to the county building in downtown Detroit. "He's wonderful. He's tremendous. I've worked for a lot of bosses, and he's the best," she gushed.

WILLIAM CRAYK

William Crayk is the cop who came in from the cold.

Livonia's chief of police—who looks more like an IBM executive in his stylish suits and distinguished silver hair—was a bricklayer by trade when he hired on with the Livonia police in August 1960.

"I thought it would be something to carry me through the winter and then I'd go back to work in the spring," says Crayk. "But the work was so interesting, I decided I'd give it another six months."

And another. And another. For four years he paid his dues in the bricklayers' union, figuring that sooner or later he'd go back to his trade of seven years. Finally, he made the big leap—he let his union card lapse and made the commitment to staying a cop.

"It's been a very interesting career. I couldn't have made a luckier choice," he says.

It took more than a bitter winter in 1959 to get him thinking about inside work. It also took an old friend with persuasive ways. Crayk and his wife, Marilyn, his childhood sweetheart, had just moved to a new Livonia subdivision. Their neighbors were friends from Detroit's Mackenzie High School.

"My friend had always wanted to be a cop, but it never entered my mind," says

Crayk. "He came over one night with an application and said, 'I'm not leaving until you fill it out.' So I filled it out. Well, he later got divorced and moved out. I got the job and here I am. But where he's at, now, I don't know; I haven't seen him since."

Crayk, 55, looks anything but the old stereotype of a suburban police chief. An avid basketball player, he is as trim as the half-miler he was in high school. (He played basketball for two years at Alma College, but dropped out of a teaching program due to lack of funds.)

He is the son of a Scottish immigrant, a ship's carpenter whose father ran the shipyard in Aberdeen. And his mother came from a long line of bricklayers, so it was natural that Crayk would get into the trades.

He still thinks of himself as a tradesman. "I rebuild the house annually and my wife puts up with it. One time she asked me to fix a shower stall and I ended up tearing the family room apart, rebuilding the kitchen, and redoing the fireplace. The whole house was torn up. So, she doesn't mention too many projects anymore."

Neither does Crayk think along the lines of police-chief stereotypes. He actually supports such Supreme Court decisions as Miranda, which required police to read suspects their rights.

"In those days [1960], they swore you in, strapped a gun on your side, and sent you out the door. You got your training on the job," he says. "We've recognized the need to improve ourselves. Supreme Court decisions have forced us to better understand ourselves, to develop a better concept of law enforcement. The Supreme Court decisions were forced upon us, but the final outcome was a better product. Officers today are more able to deal with a more complex society."

His department's growth since 1960 has reflected the city's boom. He was the 42nd member of the department. Now, there are about 150. Along the way, Crayk, past president of the Livonia Police Officers Association, negotiated the first police union contract with the city.

Along the way, too, Crayk, who became chief in 1983, has had his share of interesting cases. But despite the dangerous nature of the business, Crayk has never pulled his gun on the job. "And I hope I never do."

Respected by his peers, Livonia's top cop has been president of the Wayne County Police Chiefs and president of the Michigan Association of Public Employees Retirement Systems. Somehow, he has found time to stay active in the community, coaching kids' football, baseball, and basketball.

One of his Little League baseball players later became a cadet, then a full-fledged member of the force, specializing in computer programming.

Quite a foundation the old bricklayer has built.

RUSS SAGRIPANTI

Russ Sagripanti must never have heard that retirement is, well, a time to retire. Instead of taking it easy, the 64-year-old Livonian has spent the last three years as a tutor and author at Focus: HOPE, a successful inner-city project in Detroit that makes skilled laborers out of the unskilled and unemployed.

"I've done a lot of different things in my lifetime. This is the most meaningful," says Sagripanti, who volunteers 16 hours a week at Focus: HOPE's Machinist Training Institute. "My philosophy is society is what we make it. We have to do the best we can."

Sagripanti retired from Ford Motor Company in September 1986 after a 26-year career. He began as a janitor and ended as superintendent of operations at the Ford Research Center in Dearborn.

Focus: HOPE was founded by a Catholic priest, Rev. William Cunningham, following the 1967 riots in Detroit. It has

food, prescription, and day-care programs as well. The machinist program is housed in an old factory.

"It's an eight-month program," says Sagripanti. "Half the time is spent in the shop learning basic machine tools, basic operation. The other half is spent in a classroom.

"The payoff is when you see a student who has graduated come back announcing he or she has a meaningful job. It's the greatest feeling in the world. What all this has done is put some dignity and meaning back into their lives."

Sagripanti, a Livonia resident of 18 years, co-authored one of the training manuals used in the school, and his story as a volunteer has been used in a series of United Way commercials created to increase volunteerism. "In volunteering, you get more back than you give, by far," says Sagripanti.

Some of his successful students may beg to differ.

SUE DANIEL

Greenmead Historical Village isn't really just a one-woman operation. It just seems that way sometimes. Sue Daniel is that woman.

Greenmead is a 100-acre jewel at the very northwest corner of Livonia. The land was bought by the city in 1976 and now includes a village of nineteenth- and early twentieth-century buildings that are being restored to their original condition; community gardens where, for a modest fee, Livonians can rent plots of ground for growing vegetables and other crops; the Hill farm and museum, a splendid collection of farm buildings, carriage houses, gazebos, and a farmhouse that was widely considered the grandest farmhouse in Wayne County in the 1800s; and undeveloped woods.

ABOVE: The Shaw House has a stately new location at Greenmead, nestled among other buildings that were moved to the site to preserve the city's history. Photo by Ulrich Tutsch

RIGHT: As the primary force behind the Greenmead Historical Village, Sue Daniel continues to commit her time and energy to every facet of the preservation of the 100-acre jewel, whose buildings reflect Livonia's early history. The Michigan Stock Shop/Steve Fecht

The 15-building village could without much exaggeration be called Danielville. When the first two buildings—a country store and an interurban train waiting station from Newburgh and Ann Arbor Trail— were moved to the site in 1976, Daniel was there. When someone needed to go to the state library in Lansing or the Detroit Public Library to research how to authentically fix up and decorate the buildings, Daniel got in her car and spent hours in the stacks finding what she needed. When the huge Alexander Blue house was moved here one hot summer day and the

monstrous tractor that had been freighted in from Kentucky to do the job began springing leaks from its radiator in the middle of Newburgh Road, Daniel was up on the engine pouring in water to keep things moving.

Need someone to cajole city council for funds, there's Daniel. Need a tour guide for a school class, there's Daniel.

"I used to go skiing," she says with a laugh when asked about other hobbies. "Till I got mixed up with this. Now, there isn't much time."

Daniel has been a librarian with the Livonia Public Schools since 1969 and at Cass Elementary since 1980, which accounts for her familiarity with old history books, plat maps, and census reports. In 1973, another librarian asked Daniel to attend a meeting of the historical commission. A few months later, Daniel took over chairmanship of the restoration committee—a post she still holds—and the rest is, ahem, history. Or will be when she and her 150 or so fellow Greenmead volunteers

complete their arduous task of stripping woods, painting, rewiring, putting in heating ducts, and everything that goes into rebuilding and refurbishing buildings that go back to 1832.

"I never dreamed when I started working on the Shaw House that we'd end up working on 15 buildings. And I had no idea, of course, that there'd ever be a Greenmead," says Daniel, a Livonia resident since 1943 and a 1954 graduate of Livonia Bentley High School.

Today, Daniel is also chairman of the Historical Commission, a member of the Historical Society, and a member of the Historic Preservation Commission.

A federal judge since 1986, Patrick Duggan's most famous trial was the Ronald Bailey murder trial he oversaw as a circuit judge in Wayne County. It was his last major trial before he moved to the federal bench. The Michigan Stock Shop/ Steve Fecht

Mayor Robert Bennett was elected to office in 1987. His interests in good, honest government became evident after his election campaign. Although the city government's office holders supported his opponent, Bennett's criterion lay in job performance, not patronage, therefore allowing the department managers to keep their positions. Bennett is seen here at a 1990 Memorial Day celebration in Veterans Park. The Michigan Stock Shop/ Steve Fecht

"Sometimes I get frustrated at the process. I got close to throwing in the towel a number of times. But we knew it was going to take a long time and the speed we could do it would depend on the money we have. So, we've done it one building at a time."

Daniel says she works about 30 hours a week at Greenmead, after school or on weekends. "I enjoy it most of the time and sometimes I wonder why I'm doing it. I'm in so deep, I'm stuck with it. I have so much time into it, if I quit, I'd see that as time wasted. So I keep at it."

Progress is slow, but steady. Three acres on the south end were sold to the U.S. Postal Service for $367,000, and that will provide for an income-earning investment and some building improvements. Two part-time city employees are now at the Greenmead office. "Now, if I can just get 'em to hire someone with museum experience."

And then she's off. She has work to do. She's in the middle of a transcription of the 1860 census, which will help her decide how to decorate some of the old farmhouses at the village. And there's a book she's nearly done co-writing—*Pictorial History of Livonia.*

"We just don't have enough history here," she'd said earlier. But much more than they'd have without her.

PATRICK DUGGAN

Patrick Duggan is patriarch of the Duggan clan, a force in Livonia and Wayne County politics. The senior Duggan was named a federal judge late in 1986 and assumed the post after hearing one last circuit court trial—the infamous Ronald Bailey murder case, one of the most notorious in county history.

His son, Michael, orchestrated Edward McNamara's successful run for county executive despite being a young and recent (1983) graduate of the University of Michigan law school. It was his research paper that convinced McNamara, a white, subur-

ban mayor, that he could win the top spot in county government, and currently Michael is the county's assistant executive and point man on tough issues.

And Patrick's wife, Joan, ran a spirited and nearly successful campaign for mayor of Livonia in 1987.

Patrick Duggan wasn't one of those who knew at an early age what he wanted to do and laid out a plan to get there. "It was during my college days [at Xavier University in Ohio] that the idea of law school popped up," he says.

Maybe it was his summers spent as a teenager working long hours pitching hay and picking cucumbers on a farm in Macomb County that sowed the seeds of white-collar employment. Or maybe it was working as a soda jerk in Detroit.

But never in his wildest dreams did he envision himself a federal judge. He never thought about it much, either, in his early days in general practice with the Livonia firm of Brashear, Brashear, Mies and Duggan.

"No, I didn't," he says. "I suppose most lawyers have aspirations of becoming a judge at one time or another, but most of the time you don't think of it as realistic."

Duggan practiced law for 18 years, then was appointed to a circuit court vacancy in 1976. After winning election twice, he was appointed to a federal position by President Ronald Reagan.

"He called personally," Duggan says. "Even though I had been forewarned that he would call, nevertheless it's a big thrill when you hear the president of the United States calling you. He has that amazing ability to sound so warm and friendly. He worded it in such a manner that it was almost a favor I was doing by taking it."

The appointment capped an active career in politics and community service. He was chairman of the Livonia YMCA for two years and on its original organizing committee. He was president of the Livonia Chamber of Commerce, Livonia Bar Association, Livonia Jaycees, and Michigan Jaycees. He helped start the paralegal program at Madonna College nearly 20 years ago, and continues to teach there.

Farming's loss has been Livonia's gain.

That just barely scratches the surface of good and interesting characters in Livonia. There are the volunteers who have the new recycling program off to such a good start. And the volunteers who drive the cars in the Meals on Wheels program, delivering hot food to Livonia's sick and elderly.

Want to meet an interesting character at City Hall? Meet Ron Mardiros, the long-time city assessor who organizes the hugely successful Heart Fund each year. A former restaurant owner, Mardiros is a fount of knowledge for reporters and those interested in the workings of City Hall.

Want to meet an extraordinary politician? Meet Mayor Robert Bennett, the former Michigan Bell employee who won a hard-fought election for mayor in 1987. Why extraordinary? In other suburban communities, supporting the wrong candidate for mayor is usually a career death sentence for city employees. Not with Bennett. Even department heads who worked long and hard for his rival kept their jobs. The only criterion, they found, was job performance, not political affiliation.

Non-Livonians in Wayne County must marvel at how many Livonians hold important county positions. There's McNamara, as county executive, and Michael Duggan, as his top assistant. Another is Robert Ficano, who now that he is 38 is no longer called the boy sheriff. He got that tag when he was appointed to the post in 1983 at the age of 30. Critics said the seemingly impossible job of restoring order to the Wayne County jail and the sheriff's department would show what a foolish choice he was. Instead, he has proven them the fools and was elected to the post in 1985 and re-elected in 1988.

Or if it's savvy businesspeople you'd

like to meet, how about Betty Jean Awrey, past president of the Livonia Chamber of Commerce and vice president for the hugely successful Awrey Bakeries?

Or Jeanne Hildebrandt, manager of the roughly 900,000-square-foot Livonia Mall.

Or Jeanne Paluzzi, a long-time Livonia volunteer who found herself in the early 1970s in need of money and a job and decided to go into public relations. She was laid off from her first two jobs and fired from her third a few weeks before Christmas when a new department head came in with a stiff broom. But she persevered and today owns JGP Marketing Group, is affiliated with another firm in Windsor, Ontario, and has served as vice president of the Small Business Association of Michigan, the White House Conference on Small Business, the board of directors of the Livonia Chamber of Commerce, and the Advisory Council on Small Business of the Federal Reserve Bank in Chicago.

If it's youth you're looking for, there's Dale Weighill, who was elected at 19 to the Clarenceville Board of Education in 1989.

And Michael McGee. When Poland's communist government turned over power to Solidarity, Poland turned to America for help to finance reform and get a stagnant economy growing again. A revolutionary—bankers should pardon the expression—bond deal was put together, giving Americans the chance to invest in Poland.

Mike McGee, a Livonia resident and son of longtime *Livonia Observer* editor Marie McGee, was the bond broker who came up with the idea and who put the deal together.

"People" helped make Barbra Streisand famous. They haven't done too badly for Livonia, either.

GREAT LIVONIA PLACES

Commerce, industry, and great people are some of the necessary ingredients for a successful city, one that becomes a home for people, not just a residence or an address or a convenient place to live so they can get to and from work in a hurry.

In Livonia's 36 square miles there are dozens of parks, nature trails, ball fields, golf courses, and wonderful places that help define this as an exemplary place to live. Come, let's take a seasonal tour of just a few of them:

EARLY JANUARY: HINES PARK

Hines Park meanders for 20 miles, from Plymouth on the west to Dearborn on the east. It twists and turns, loops this way and that, paralleling the Middle Rouge River that bisects it.

Edward Hines Drive runs from one end of the park to the other, right through the floodplain. Where the floodplain is narrow, so, too, is the park. Where the floodplain widens out, there are baseball diamonds, toboggan hills, beach volleyball sites, and picnic areas.

For 3½ miles the park runs through the south end of Livonia. The park is gorgeous in the summertime, of course, with climax forests thick with green and the sound of softball players filling the air with despair or joy, depending on the game situation. Cars fill the road and parking lots. Joggers and bicyclists share the asphalt bike path. Squirrels jabber overhead and if you look

Crowds of 25,000 or more always flock each June to Greenmead's Arts and Crafts Festival, one of the best in the area. Photo by Gary Quesada/Korab Ltd.

real close, you can spot hawks, possums, raccoons, beavers, and deer.

But some would say the prettiest time of year in the park is on a pristine clear day in winter, with the temperature so low your breath seems to crystalize as you exhale. The crowds are gone, traffic is at a minimum, and there's a peace in the air that makes it seem impossible that this part of the park is in a city of 104,000.

At the west end of Livonia, abutting Plymouth, snow glistens along the rolling hills. A solitary runner in wool mask and mittens zips by. Newburgh Lake, created by the dam at Newburgh Road to the east, runs along the road to the south. A dozen kids play hockey on the lake, half a mile away, the shishshing of their skates easily cutting through the cold air. Past them, eight ice fishermen sit on crates, waiting for perch or sunfish to hit on the larvae they're using as bait.

A gorgeous stone bathroom and rest station—a remnant from a turn-of-the-century affluence of workmanship when even bathrooms were built to last, and with class—sits at the tip of Newburgh Point back from the road, on a hill overlooking the lake. Up a ways, the fishermen have parked their cars on Sumac Trail, thick with sumacs, oak trees, and, in the spring, the sweet scent of lilacs.

East of Newburgh Road, the park nar-

rows down as the river, thin here, leaves the lake behind. The woods are thick. Fallen trees form dams and rapids as the river goes through its contortions. At Joy, near Farmington, at the southern edge of the city, hundreds of ducks—mallards, Pekings, and ring-necks—and a dozen majestic Canada geese feast side by side on breadsticks and carrots dropped off by some bird lover.

The river opens out here into another small lake and hundreds more ducks float placidly on the water. No need migrating when life is so sweet here. A car pulls up and a family—mom, dad, and a boy of about eight—get out of the car and approach the birds. Many of the ducks run into the lake. Some stay. None of the geese leave. Bold, cantankerous, and confident, this family holds no fear for them. They do hold bread crumbs and soon the ducks in the water are clambering back up the banks.

EARLY MAY: LADBROKE DETROIT RACE COURSE

Horses. They are poetic and prosaic: writers praise them, cowboys and farmers tame them. They have tilled our fields, carried us to war and pervaded our culture. At DRC they fuel dreams of riches, and if not riches, then at least a payoff big enough to break even on the day.

Michigan's only thoroughbred race track is a good place for betting, and a great place for people-watching and maybe playing a little hooky from the office.

The track is one place where there is no illiteracy. Everyone reads the *Racing Form*—studies it—scanning the small type and letters for clues and signs.

Horse racing is the sport of kings, but the court isn't all regal. For every elegant woman in a dress there are several guys in shorts and black socks with tattoos on their arms; for every businessman in a suit, there are several someones in jeans. They are united by a common language.

"C'mon six. Six horse. Easy ride on the six. C'MON SIX," chants a young man staring at a TV yards away from the ticket window. The open-air seats are a great place between races, as the warm sun feels so soothing after a Michigan winter, but with the track a mile around and the horses on the backside, those without binoculars race to the TV sets scattered around the clubhouse and grandstand for a better view of reality. (Another fine spot is down along the rail, watching the horses loosen up before the start. Later, in the swelter of summer, the air conditioned clubhouse is the place to be.)

It doesn't matter that the six is moving backward in the pack like he's on an escalator going the wrong way. "C'mon six. C'mon six," the young man chants.

A man in a silk tie asks a character in a T-shirt who's chomping on a short cigar: "Did you get that jockey change in the sixth?" There are no strangers here. Millionaires who own companies in the nearby industrial zone trade tips with track hangers-on. People who arrived in Mercedes stand shoulder to shoulder with Detroiters who arrived by bus.

THIS is Livonia's melting pot. Folks are united or divided by the numbers on their bet slips, nothing else. Who you are and what you own are temporarily irrelevant. The surge of 10 throroughbreds pounding down the backstretch as the crowd goes wild is all that matters.

Dead tickets litter the floor and aisles like ticker-tape confetti. Excuses rain down as fast as the tickets. "I was gonna bet the one, too." "I had the five till the last minute." "Hey, who touted me off the seven?" "What kind of a ride was that. The best horse in the race and he rides him like that?"

Matt Barge, the favorite, finishes in a photo finish in the night race with a 49-1 longshot. Talk about long tension. Do you win $3 for a $2 bet, or do you win $96? It's Barge! . . . Wait, there's been a protest. Both bets are still alive. Hunt for the long-shot ticket you dumped on the floor. Sweat a few more thumbtacks. And, then, it's official: Barge.

Another race and the day is done. Winners tell jokes and laugh. Losers say, "Deal." Except that the cards have all been played; there are no more races. It's 7 p.m. and time to go.

MID-JUNE: THE ANNUAL ARTS AND CRAFTS FESTIVAL, GREENMEAD
More than 25,000 people will stream through the grounds this weekend at Greenmead, in the northwest corner of Livonia, to admire—and buy—the wares of about 250 crafters.

Pottery, quilts, paintings, jewelry, ceramics—cheap and expensive—lure the throngs. But the biggest jewel of them all is what surrounds them: Greenmead and the Greenmead Historical Village.

The city purchased the 100-acre site in 1976, and in the fall of that year, the first two buildings were moved to the village, which is home now to 15 buildings. Some have been completely restored and furnished. Others are in various states of repair as volunteers donate their time and labor to do all the tedious, time-consuming tasks needed to restore buildings long in decline.

Livonia's history goes back to the early nineteenth century, and Greenmead reflects that. Come, take a quick tour on the semicircular road that the village has been placed along.

This tour—and all tours, which cost two dollars for adults, one dollar for seniors, and nothing for kids—begins at the Cranson-Hinbern house, where the administrative offices and souvenir shop are located.

ABOVE LEFT: Traditions hold sway at Ladbroke Detroit Race Course, including a bugler calling the horses to the post. The Michigan Stock Shop/ Steve Fecht

ABOVE RIGHT: The paddock area at Ladbroke DRC is a fine place for people-watching when owners, handlers, grooms, and jockeys gear up for the big moment. The Michigan Stock Shop/Steve Fecht

RIGHT: The railbirds study the Racing Form and look for a big payoff—or at least enough to break even for the day at Ladbroke DRC. The Michigan Stock Shop/ Steve Fecht

ABOVE: It's a battle to the finish, with just a head separating one horse from another, and the happy bettors from the losers. The Michigan Stock Shop/ Steve Fecht

FAR LEFT: A keen eye for horse flesh always helps as post time approaches. The Michigan Stock Shop/ Steve Fecht

LEFT: The race is done, the battle lost or won, as the jockey dismounts and attends to his ride. The Michigan Stock Shop/Steve Fecht

The Cranson family built the back of the house in 1832 and the front was added on in the 1850s. The Hinberns bought the house in the early 1900s and owned it until the Southland Corporation bought it for a 7-Eleven at Seven Mile and Inkster. It was moved to Greenmead in 1985 and opened in 1987.

Just up the road is the Kingsley House. Nathan Kingsley arrived in the area with his parents in the 1830s and he built this house when he was married in 1843. A cast-iron cook stove in the kitchen was all that heated the home in the winter; surprisingly, many of the Greek Revival homes of the time were built without fireplaces.

Next door is the Shaw House. Thomas Shaw never meant to settle here; he was passing through in 1836 on his way to Indiana and was caught here for three days in a series of storms. He liked what he saw, bought some land for a farm, and built the house in 1843 on the site of what is now a cloverleaf of the I-275 freeway on Six Mile. This is the first house volunteers worked on and it was moved here in 1981.

Next to it is the Blue office, a building Alexander Blue used for an office to run his extensive farm on Middlebelt. Then comes the Newburg school, the parsonage, and the Newburg church, part of a series of buildings at the east end of the village that were moved here from the intersection of Ann Arbor Trail and Newburgh; they are being restored to the period of 1910-1925, when that was a thriving corner of Livonia.

The church has been completed and the school, which was built in 1861 and used until 1922, was finished in 1989.

Tucked in to the south, behind the Newburgh and Ann Arbor Trail buildings, is the huge Blue house, named not for its color but for the family that owned it. The house was moved here in 1986 in a day filled with drama. One moving company got the house up on blocks, then decided it was too big to move and quit the project. Eventually a company from Kentucky came in and got the house rolling ever so slowly up Middlebelt, then over to Newburgh, and up Newburgh to Greenmead.

On the way up Newburgh, the radiator on the huge tractor doing the pulling sprouted a bunch of leaks. If the engine blew on the tractor, the house would have sat in the middle of the busy thoroughfare for days, while a replacement tractor was found somewhere in the country and shipped here.

Frantically, moving company workers and Greenmead volunteers filled jugs of water borrowed from neighbors along the way to pour into the radiator and on the engine. Somehow, the tractor kept rolling and the house finally made it to its site after nearly a full day en route.

A bungalow sits next to the general store, awaiting much-needed renovation. The store, though, is a masterpiece. "A.J. Geer," the sign out front announces. "General Store, dry goods, hardware, groceries."

Inside, an old checker board and wood checkers sit atop a wooden barrel, waiting patiently for play to resume. Long wooden counters run the length of the store. Behind them, canned goods, Quaker Oat barrels, and New Era potato chip cannisters fill the shelves. That stuff isn't for sale;

other stuff is—yo-yos (75 cents), slate blackboards (50 cents), whistles (25 cents), and kazoos (40 cents), for example.

Next door is the waiting station for the interurban railroad that used to run out from Detroit, and next to that is a Quaker meeting house.

The village takes up just 10 acres or so of the Greenmead site. On a larger plot of ground to the west sits the old Simmons farm and Hill House Museum.

Joshua Simmons bought the land in 1824, 11 years before Livonia Township was established and 13 years before Michigan became a state. He went back to New York, saved up his money, and returned in 1826 with his new wife. He built the farmhouse in 1841. Attorney Sherwin Hill purchased the farm in 1920 and raised cattle until his death in 1961. The property was placed on the National Register of Historic Places in 1971.

The Simmons farm includes two carriage houses, greenhouse, farm-hand house, chicken coop, caretaker cottage, gazebo, and the wonderful farmhouse, with its many huge rooms, fabulous kitchen, and four fireplaces.

In its day, it was known far and wide as the grandest farmhouse in Wayne County. (In the 1930s, heavyweight champion Joe Louis liked it here so much, he'd come out here and train for big bouts.)

The farm property includes the Hill House Gardens, which are tended by volunteers and are open to the public during daylight hours.

A third area at Greenmead much in use is the Community Gardens, a cleared five-acre tract of land where, for a nominal fee, Livonia residents can rent a plot of land for a summer vegetable garden.

Behind the gardens are 40 acres of woods and fields, which serve as a greenbelt for the Victor Corporate Park being built to the south. Ideas being tossed around for the 40 acres include a working farm, camp grounds for kids, in-

terurban railway track and working train, and picnic area.

Greenmead: great name, great place.

LATE JUNE: SPREE, FORD FIELD

Most places, you have a birthday, people do a little singing, maybe buy a present, cut a little cake. When Livonia celebrates a birthday, the whole town turns out for six days of fireworks, sports competition, parades, clowns, gobs of food, bed races, midway rides, tigers jumping through hoops, tugs-o-war, and much, much more.

Traffic forms a near-gridlock, but no one seems to mind. Shuttle buses bring in spectators and participants from the parking lot at City Hall, or folks just pull over their car where they can find a legal spot and walk on in.

Tuesday—the circus opens; pig races; magic show; baseball and softball; and a pizza jamboree.

Wednesday—more circus; more softball and baseball; soothe your throat at the beer tent.

Thursday—parade; outdoor concert; polka at the beer tent; carbo load at the spaghetti dinner.

RIGHT: The Newburg Church, built in 1861 and restored in 1989 after 67 years of disuse, is once again a place to begin a life together, as this local couple found out. The Michigan Stock Shop/Steve Fecht

FACING PAGE, TOP LEFT: Some may think pigs are slow and ungainly until they see the speedy swine dash around the track at Spree's hilarious pig race. The Michigan Stock Shop/Steve Fecht

FACING PAGE, TOP RIGHT: A Ferris wheel, a roller coaster, games, and carnival treats such as caramel apples entice youngsters at Spree. Photo by Gary Quesada/ Korab Ltd.

FACING PAGE, BOTTOM: The old-fashioned carousel is always a hit for young and old at Spree. The Michigan Stock Shop/Steve Fecht

Friday—special rides for the handicapped; opening ceremonies for the Corporate Cup athletic challege; tug-o-war; scholarship presentations; professional entertainment.

Saturday—Corporate Cup competition at nearby Bentley High School track and pool; finals of the senior citizen softball tourney; Big Wheel races for the kids; bed race; rock 'n' roll oldies but goldies.

Sunday—pancake breakfast; chili cook-off; lip-sync contest; last, and most certainly not least, the fireworks.

Spree! Whee!

Late July: Veterans Park

Michigan is a hotbed for runners and road running, with races every weekend of the year one place or another. Over the years, the Roadrunner Classic in Livonia has earned the reputation as one of those races you just can't miss.

The energy begins to build about 3 p.m. as volunteers gather to put up banners and balloons, get the food out and the grills ready, put out the cones and markers on the course, and attend to the myriad details that go into a great race. Every

race, it seems, has its screw-ups; not this one. Hosted by veteran runners for veteran runners, from start to finish this is a night to remember. (The race director is Doug Kurtis, a 1970 graduate of Livonia Stevenson High School and a former Michigan State University runner; in 1989, Kurtis set a world record by breaking two hours and 20 minutes in 12 different marathons, from Barcelona to Bangkok.)

6 p.m.—Hundreds of kids and their parents, and some adult speedburners as well, gather at the starting line for the one-mile run. Kids as young as three—their race numbers covering their chest and belly—bounce nervously from foot to foot awaiting the start. The Moslem Highlanders belt out chilling, inspiring tunes on their bagpipes and drums a few yards away. "BOOM" goes the starting gun and off they go, the kids racing off at a pace they can never maintain and then getting passed by the adults, who have done this before and know to pace themselves.

The runners circle the softball fields, baseball diamond, and Eddie Edgar Ice Arena, returning to the cheers of hundreds of fans lining the street at the finish line. Duane Zemens of Detroit wins the mile in 5:23. It is the first race he has ever won. Normally no awards are given for the mile, but when race organizers learn that Zemens attended his father's funeral earlier in the day, they find a trophy for him.

6:30—"BOOM!" And the runners are off for the eight-kilometer (4.96 miles) race. From Indiana and Ohio, from Traverse City and Flint, from Sarnia, Ontario, and Windsor they have come, 1,500 runners from throughout the state and the Midwest who have learned that Livonia is the place to be on the last Saturday in July.

Kathy Hadler, an All-American from the University of Tennessee, breaks the course record for the women. Van Savell of Ann Arbor breaks the course record for the men. For another hour runners and race walkers stream across the finish line and then the real fun begins.

7-11:30—Runners cool down from their steamy run through Livonia streets by hosing off under an outdoor shower. Then they head to the food (hot dogs, yogurt, fruit) and the refreshments (kegs of beer and pop). A disc jockey belts out dance tunes on the public-address system. A thousand or more dancers fill the parking lot next to the YMCA and boogie the night away.

One of them is Susan Tatigian, a Michigan State runner and daughter of city attorney Harry Tatigian. Another is city councilman Ron Ochala. Awards are passed out in the various age groups. Hula dancers take the stage. Wheelchair racers dance in their chairs, rocking from one wheel to the other. Some dance with others in chairs; some dance with able-bodied runners.

Too soon, another Roadrunner Classic is history.

THE LAST WEDNESDAY IN AUGUST:
WHISPERING WILLOWS, FOX CREEK,
AND IDYL WYLD GOLF COURSES
This is the day that proves, more than any other, that Livonia is a city with a heart. Area golfers—from perfect swingers with 1-handicaps to complete duffers who think a driver is the fellow behind the wheel of the golf cart—take part in the annual Ben Celani Golf Day Benefit, the major fundraiser for the Heart Fund.

About 700 golfers take their turns teeing off, though that is hardly the end of the festivities. Nearly 1,200 will participate in one event or another.

Think you're good at bocce ball? Compete with 150 or so other players for the first prize of $750.

Want to ogle celebrities? Look, there's Chuck Daly, the coach of the Detroit Pistons. And isn't that Jacques Demers, the coach of the Red Wings hockey team? Past attendees have included ex-Tigers Mickey Lolich, Paul Foytack, and Ray Herbert; Piston Vinnie Johnson; former

Detroit Red Wing hockey players Billy Dea, Jimmy Peters, and Bill Gadsby; and Hall of Fame football player Dick (Night Train) Lane.

When all the proceeds had been totaled up, the Heart Fund had raised $145,530 in 1989, and had surpassed one million dollars in its first 12 years.

Before the day is over, more than 3,600 Hygrade Ball Park franks (made in Livonia but made famous at Tiger Stadium) will be served. More than 850 steaks and 250 chicken breasts will be eaten. More than 1,000 ice cream bars will cool things off. A few bottles of beer will wash it all down.

Ron Mardiros, the longtime city assessor, Heart Fund president, and person who puts the golf day together, ought to consider charity fund-raising as a second career.

The common folks show up—those who need a nametag—as well as most of Wayne County's high society, intelligentsia, politicians, and judiciary.

With some fund-raisers, a lot of people send in a check and count their blessings they didn't have to go in person. Not this day.

There's lots of golf, of course. Then there's the bocce tournament; putting, driving, and basketball contests; a card room; food; liquid refreshments; a barbershop; manicures; handwriting analysis by Al

RIGHT: Each spring, residents attending Spree, Livonia's annual birthday bash/extravaganza, enjoy six days of carnival rides, great food, parades, softball tournaments, pig races, and fireworks. Photo by Gary Quesada/Korab Ltd.

BELOW: The Wilson Barn is not only a historic site; it is also a great place to shop for fresh produce, thanks to a thriving farmers' market. The Michigan Stock Shop/ Steve Fecht

BELOW RIGHT: About 1,500 runners gather on the last Saturday evening in July each summer for the Roadrunner Classic, a five-mile race through the streets of Livonia. The run is a classic, and the party after is even better. The Michigan Stock Shop/ Steve Fecht

Wood; caricatures by Irv Tasco; fortune-telling by Gypsy Dee; and, in keeping with the name of the charity, cholesterol and blood-pressure checks.

The golf day is named for Ben Celani, one of the Heart Fund organizers, who later died of a heart attack. It is held in his honor and in honor of two other heart attack victims who were active in the community—Nick Canzano and Chuck Ledgerwood. Though the trauma room at St. Mary Hospital has received the largest sum of money to date—$503,000—the fund is spread throughout the area.

More than $200,000 has gone to scholarships for Livonia high school students to attend the University of Michigan, Madonna College, Schoolcraft College, Michigan State University, and Eastern Michigan University.

ABOVE: The Middle Rouge River flows through southern Livonia and bisects beautiful Hines Park, which meanders through 20 miles of floodplain. The Michigan Stock Shop/Steve Fecht

Other beneficiaries have included the Special Olympics, Felician Sisters Mother House, Friends of Wilson Barn, Livonia Goodfellows, Friends of the Library, Angela Hospice, Kiwanis, Association for Retarded Citizens, Livonia Symphony Orchestra, Drug Abuse Resistance Education, and many others.

In addition to the funds raised and the good times, there is the generous contribution of area businesspeople, which nearly eliminates the overhead. Sponsors honored at the 1989 Heart Fund Awards Night at City Hall in December included Joe Maiorana, owner of Joe's Produce on Seven Mile, and Scott Grace, owner of the Daly's Drive-In on Plymouth, for their gifts of food.

"The Heart Fund raises the spirit of this community," says Mayor Robert Bennett. "It raises the level of involvement in this community. And it raises the pride in this community."

But wouldn't it be better to hold it on the weekend, on a Saturday or Sunday? Not on your life, says Mardiros. "We always hold it on Wednesday. You know how doctors always have Wednesday off? Well, when we started out, we didn't want them to have any excuses for not coming, so we

held it on their day off," Mardiros says with a laugh.

After all, he's got to make sure they're properly assessed.

LATE NOVEMBER: THE ROPERTI TURKEY FARM ON FIVE MILE ROAD

'Tis the Friday before Thanksgiving and all through the Roperti Turkey Farm workers scurry around.

It's killing day out back. Inside the farmhouse, phones ring off the hook with customers placing orders.

In an era of fears over pesticides and antibiotics, and of the attraction to natural foods, it seems as if everyone is looking for a corn-fed, free-ranging turkey.

"Hello, Roperti Turkey Farm," says Jeannette McCarthy, the office organizer who keeps track by computer of customer orders and turkeys by weight. "What size turkey would you like?"

"Hello, thank you so much for calling. Can I help you?" says Christine Roperti, the farm's owner, grabbing another line.

"Roperti's, please hold," says McCarthy, who goes back to her first caller. "I've got something 16 to 18 pounds, so let's not quibble over a pound."

"Of course they're fresh. They're killed the day before you pick 'em up. We take pride in our turkeys," says Christine.

"I got good news for you—I can get you a tom instead of a hen." And, "Sure, they're worth it. We don't stick 'em with hypodermic needles under the skin to make 'em weigh more. You can come out and watch our turkeys grow every day."

Roperti's the name; turkey's the game; and anyone who has ever sunk his teeth into one on Thanksgiving Day will tell you there's nothing like it.

At $1.98 a pound, it isn't cheap. It's about double what you'd pay at a supermarket. But that would be like comparing domestic champagne to Dom Perignon. One's fine; the other is, well, Dom Perignon.

A turkey farm in Livonia in 1990 is the perfect anachronism. There are just two farms left in what used to be a farming community, and Roperti's is the only real working farm.

Roperti's parents, Tom and Mary, moved to Livonia in 1942. When they started the farm in 1948, it was surrounded by farms.

Now, it is surrounded by a five-lane road and new subdivisions. The farm's 4½ acres is assessed at $40,000 an acre and would likely be worth more than that to a developer.

When Tom and Mary died within a few weeks of each other in the summer of 1988—he was driving a tractor right until the end—speculation was that Christine would give in to development pressure, take the money and run.

Those doing the speculating didn't know Christine. She says a farm it is and a farm it shall remain. Period. Next topic.

"My dad came here in 1942 when he knew absolutely nothing," says Christine. "When my dad came here, there was nothing. Just woods and fields. My dad and I were really close. He started from nothing and he knew nothing. And I am going to keep it. He was 87 years old and still driving the tractor. Sell? Forget it."

As the phones ring, her sons, Tony and Tom, her number one hand, Wesley Bates, and several others are out back in the main building getting ready for the deluge of customers on Saturday and Sunday. There are 13 tubs in the building, each six to eight feet long, three feet wide, and three feet deep. Tomorrow, they will be filled with cold water and dead turkeys.

Today, it's killing time. But there are no bloody axes and birds running around the yard with their heads chopped off. The turkeys are hung on hooks and electrocuted. There's one machine that quickly strips the birds of feathers, but the gutting and cleaning process is labor intensive.

A trickle of customers comes in on Fri-

day. Outside, 5,000 turkeys huddle against the cold. A few yards away the stubble of what's left of the cornfields sticks out of the hard ground. The birds arrived at the farm as six-week-olds at the end of July; since then they've had the run of the place and all the corn and oats they can eat.

"They gotta be corn fed. If they're not corn fed, they're nothing," brags Christine.

Back in the house, McCarthy continues at the phone, sweet-talking customers into getting an extra pound or two. "The hardest part of working here is waiting till Thanksgiving," she says between calls. "I just CANNOT wait."

This is just a few days and a few places in Livonia. It's hard to hit all the sights on a single tour. We missed a football game Friday night at perennial power Livonia Stevenson. We missed a girl's tournament basketball game at state-ranked Livonia Ladywood, where they bomb in three-pointers like the guys and weave their offensive patterns maybe a little bit better. We missed the action at a city council meeting when something on the agenda has one neighborhood or another up in arms and democracy cooking. We missed the wonderfully restored Wilson Barn on Middlebelt. So much to see, so little time, not enough pages.

THE SPORTING LIFE

Sports is a way of life in Livonia. Here's a sampling:

Item: Stevenson High School has, year in and year out, one of the most successful varsity football programs in the state. Jack Reardon, with 25 years as head coach, is an institution in the community. In 1988, when the team fell to 4-5, it was the first losing season in 17 years. Yet, these days, Stevenson has a hard time getting enough boys to fill out a varsity and junior varsity squad. The problem? The school's soccer program is the best in the state, with state titles in 1982, 1985, 1986, and 1988. Soccer is the sport everyone wants to get into these days.

Despite the fact that the soccer team was defending state champion, despite the fact that it was 12-2-2 in its first 16 games, and despite the fact that Stevenson had won seven previous district titles in the state tournament, when it came to the district finals in 1989, guess who was an underdog? Stevenson. And to whom? None other than its inter-city arch rival, Churchill, which was top-ranked in the state and undefeated. (Think they take soccer seriously in Livonia?) Stevenson pulled off a 3-2 upset and advanced to the regionals.

Item: Schoolcraft College's women's soccer team won the National Junior College Athletic Association national championship in the fall of 1988. Not to be outdone, the women's volleyball team won the national championship the next year.

Item: Also not to be outdone, Livonia

Livonia Stevenson's soccer program is the best in the state. These members of the women's soccer team exhibit confidence and enthusiasm just before winning the final game that rewarded them with the 1990 state championship title. Photo by Gary Quesada/Korab Ltd.

Ladywood's volleyball team won the Michigan Class A girls' volleyball title in 1988 and 1989. (Ladywood is usually a powerhouse in basketball, too; in 1984, one of its players, Lisa Wagner, was named the top basketball player in a basketball-mad state and went on to play Division I basketball for Stanford University.)

Item: Doug Kurtis, a 1970 Livonia Stevenson graduate, is the race director for the Roadrunner Classic road race each summer. Though he was 37 in 1989 and held down a full-time job as a computer specialist at Ford Motor Company's world headquarters, Kurtis set a world record by running 12 marathons, each of them under two hours and 20 minutes. And he set American age records in the half marathon and at eight kilometers. Participants at the Classic include Susan Tatigian, daughter of the longtime city attorney, Harry Tatigian, and Ron Ochala, a Livonia realtor and member of the city council.

Item: The city hosts an annual seniors' slow pitch softball tournament each summer as part of its Spree birthday celebration. When it says "senior," it means senior. To qualify for this tournament, you have to have turned at least 55 on June 1. The city helps sponsor three senior teams of its own: two for 55 and over, and one for 70 and over. And interest is high enough in this tourney in the Detroit area that the field is restricted to the first 16 teams.

Item: The richest horse race in Michigan, the Michigan Mile, is held each summer at Ladbroke DRC. Ladbroke is an English sports firm; when it chose to invest in the United States, it chose Livonia's Detroit Race Course, the only thoroughbred track in the state. There's nothing like a spring day down with the railbirds, the sun warming your face, the smell of hay in your nostrils, the sleek horses so close as they warm up you can almost reach out and touch them. You can also bet on the track on such famous races as the Kentucky Derby, Preakness, and Belmont Stakes, then watch those races on one of the many TVs throughout the grandstand and clubhouse.

Item: The Livonia Collegiate Baseball League is one of the toughest in the nation, filled with college players keeping sharp over the summer and honing their skills for possible careers in the pros. The city's top team, Walter's Home Appliance, in 1989 made it to the All-American Amateur Baseball Tournament in Johnstown, Pennsylvania, and won three games before being eliminated. It was the team's 14th appearance in the national tourney.

Item: The city had two municipal, 18-hole golf courses, which is two more than most cities in the area have. Yet, it was hardly enough. Livonia opened a third, Fox Creek, in June 1988 and nearly 40,000 rounds were played there in 1989.

In Livonia, it's almost as if God had said, "Go forth and recreate."

CORPORATE CUP

The first Corporate Cup competition was held in 1987, and it immediately established itself as a community highlight, uniting members of company teams in a friendly but extremely competitive series of athletic events over a two-day period.

What is nice about the competition is the unifying effect it has, both inter-company and intra-company. It brings together people from a business who until then might only have known each other as faces in a lunchroom or across a busy office. And it brings together people from widely different companies who may not have known each other at all. By the end of the two days, friendships have been cemented, business contacts have been made, and goodwill—at the expense of a bad back or plenty of sore muscles—has been created.

In the past, teams have included the Observer & Eccentric Newspapers, Livonia YMCA, Enterprise Rent-A-Car, General Motors Hydramatic, MetroVision, Corporate Services Inc., Livonia Village Dental, Unisys, Action Distributing, Livonia Public Schools, Manufacturer's Bank, Inland-Fisher, St. Mary Hospital, and Michigan Bell.

The Cup is contested in June as part of the city's annual Spree week, which celebrates Livonia's birthday. A not-so-serious cheerleading competition, a definitely-not-serious tricycle race, and a grueling and very serious co-ed tug-of-war kick things off on Friday night.

Saturday's action includes a three-mile race and a one-mile prediction run, both through a subdivision near the field; a 440-yard relay on the track; an obstacle course involving hula-hoops, inner tubes, running around pylons, and grabbing balls; 200-yard relays in the pool nearby for both men's and women's teams; a 200-yard co-ed swimming relay; and hilarious inner tube and inflatable boat relays that leave both participants and spectators crying with laughter.

(A past winner for the women in the three-mile run and always a contender is Marybeth Dillon, a writer for the Observer Newspapers, who finished sixth in the Irish Olympic Marathon Trials in 1988.)

A softball tournament is held prior to the weekend but counts in the standings. Though a relatively young event, the Corporate Cup has already become a be-there-or-be-square highlight of summer.

GOLF

Golf is a passion throughout Michigan, from the fine Publinx courses to the dozens of private courses to the dozens of the gorgeous and challenging (and expensive) tourist courses in the northwest corner of the state that bill themselves as "America's Summer Golf Destination."

Livonians are lucky. Some municipalities have one city-owned course. Livonia is an exception; it has three. So residents don't have to drive up north; they don't have to belong to a costly private club; they don't have to wait on the throngs in line at the Publinx courses in Wayne County. They can just tote their bags across the street or get in the car and make a two-minute drive for some of the best golfing around.

Much of the impetus for Livonia's heavy involvement with municipal golf came from Ed McNamara, formerly the mayor and now Wayne County's chief executive. In the mid-1930s, when he was 10 or 12, McNamara rode his bike out to Idyl Wyld (at Five Mile, east of Levan) and, after lying about his age, got a job caddying at the then-private course. His first bag was for a guy who hit nine balls into the rough in nine consecutive holes. McNamara couldn't find any of them.

Finally, the guy was out of balls and quit for the day. He handed two quarters to McNamara and said: "You weren't worth it." Three decades later, at McNamara's prodding, the city spent one million dollars to buy it.

As a city council member in the late

RIGHT: From softball to soccer to pick-up hoops, joining in a casual game is always easy in Livonia. The Michigan Stock Shop/Steve Fecht

BELOW: John Stymelski Veterans Park is just one of 54 in Livonia, which boasts more than 1,800 acres of parkland. The Michigan Stock Shop/ Steve Fecht

LEFT: When it's too cold and too white to golf, Livonians strap on their skis and go cross-country skiing on the golf courses or in the parks. They can also take their skates or fishing poles to Newburgh Lake in Hines Park. Photo by Balthazar Korab

1960s, McNamara pushed for the city to buy the 120 acres needed to build Whispering Willows, in the far northwest corner of the city at Eight Mile and Newburgh. Mayor Harvey Moelke vehemently opposed the purchase, which ran about $3,000 an acre. With land going for $40,000 or so an acre in the area now, the purchase was a steal.

In 1988, with both courses filled to capacity and making money for the city, Livonia opened its third course, Fox Creek, at Seven Mile west of Wayne.

In 1989, the courses brought in more than $1.2 million in revenue; more than 60,000 rounds were played at Whispering Willows, more than 50,000 at Idyl Wyld, and more than 38,000 at Fox Creek.

Activities included 28 leagues, youth clinics, the Observer & Eccentric golf tournament, the hugely successful Heart Fund all-day outing at the three courses, the DARE anti-drug golf outing, youth and senior tournaments, and thousands of lessons.

And the advent of a harsh Michigan winter doesn't mean an end to activities; groomed and marked cross-country ski trails, used by thousands, are open for free at all three courses, and there is sledding on the hill at Fox Creek.

SKIING

If it's downhill skiing you're after, Mount Brighton is just 40 minutes away, west on I-96, and Alpine Valley and Mount Holly are just slightly farther away. Up north, a four-hour drive up I-75, are dozens of the finest ski resorts in the Midwest, many of them at the same complexes that offer such wonderful golf courses and views in the summer. The land up north was churned into hills and valleys by the glaciers and, combined with snows off Lake Michigan, is a haven for winter-sports enthusiasts.

PARKS AND RECREATION

Livonia's parks and recreation department is arguably the finest in metropolitan Detroit. It offers residents a diversity other communities can only dream of.

For example, the department oversees 54 parks totaling more than 1,800 acres, 77 baseball or softball diamonds, 45 tennis courts, two indoor ice arenas, four outdoor skating rinks, three outdoor pools, 18 soccer fields, 21 playgrounds, and two fitness and nature trails.

And that's just a list of places. Activities in 1989 included 20 different team sports with more than 12,000 participants playing more than 5,000 games on one or more of the 432 teams.

There were men's, women's, and co-ed slow pitch softball; modified softball; women's fast pitch softball; youth softball; hardball leagues from leagues for little kids right on through some of the top leagues in the nation for college ball players; men's basketball; men's and women's volleyball; girls' basketball; floor hockey; softball for seniors over 55; and softball for seniors over 70.

Age certainly wasn't a factor. Tots played T-ball; 80-year-olds made fine running catches on line drives up the gap. The season didn't matter, either. While summer was the busiest time of year, of course, 92 teams were involved in various sports during the winter.

The Detroit area has turned out many National Hockey League players over the last 10 years, including NHL All-Stars such as Al Iafrate of Livonia. A main reason is available ice and good teams. Again, age isn't a factor: mites of six and seven can find a team, and so can aging veterans in the over-30, no-checking leagues. Surprising to some, there is even a league for girls.

The Devon Aire Arena is on West Chicago at Henry Ruff roads. The other arena, Eddie Edgar Arena, is tucked into the city's main sports complex just southwest of City Hall. When not in use for hockey during summer months, the arena, which holds 1,500, is used for concerts, festivals, and as a staging area for the annual Spree, the city's week-long birthday celebration.

The arena is named for one of the city's most illustrious former residents. Eddie Edgar was a star sports reporter in the heyday of old-time journalism. A character right out of *The Front Page,* Edgar worked for the *Detroit Free Press* in the days when telegraph operators sat in the news room banging out stories in Morse code.

Edgar started work in Detroit in 1924, being introduced to his sports editor, Harry Bullion, as Bullion was tossing a phone out the window because he didn't like the call. Bullion asked Edgar what the W.W. stood for in front of his last name. "Wilson William," Edgar replied.

"Not here it isn't," snapped Bullion, who said he wasn't going to have anyone on his staff with such a sissy name. So, Edgar decided to call himself Eddie and a legend was begun. He later was named to the Michigan Amateur Sports Hall of Fame and was a charter member of the University of Michigan Media Hall of Fame. He spotted Joe Louis as an amateur boxer and helped start him on his career. He could regale listeners for hours with tales of the old Brown Bomber, or old power-boat drivers, or members of the Detroit Tigers who have long since gone into the Hall of Fame.

Not ever ready for retirement, Edgar went to work in 1964 as a sports and general assignment reporter and columnist for the Observer & Eccentric newspapers, a chain of 13 highly successful, twice-a-week suburban newspapers headquartered in Livonia, and was still active there

until shortly before his death. Edgar worked almost up to the day he died at 88 in 1986. He holds a record that probably will never be broken by having attended more than 60 consecutive opening days for the Detroit Tigers. Edgar, a 48-year resident of Livonia and one of those who pushed for its incorporation as a city in 1950, was the oldest journalist in Michigan when he died and possibly the oldest sports reporter in the world.

If the major sports like softball, baseball, hockey, basketball, or golf don't turn you on, maybe one of the minor sports will. There are plenty to choose from in Livonia as the Parks and Recreation Department has affiliations with a judo club, a boxing club, and a ski club and offers programs in figure skating, bowling, and roller skating.

And if you're not sure what turns you on but would like to find out, you can sign up for lessons in skiing, tennis, swimming, and golf.

Again, most communities are thrilled to call one swimming pool their own. Not Livonia. The city has three municipal pools to fight the 90 degree temperatures and 90 percent humidity that Michiganders learn

RIGHT: Golf is a passion in Michigan. The city owns three fine, 18-hole courses, including the Whispering Willows course, seen here. The Michigan Stock Shop/ Steve Fecht

BELOW: The University of Michigan's mighty football team is annually ranked in the Top Ten. Livonia residents are just 35 minutes away. The Michigan Stock Shop/Erdvilas Bankauskas

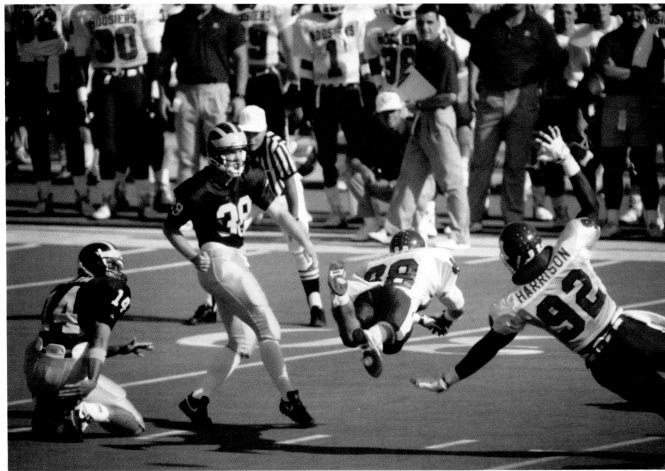

BELOW: For Livonia's major league baseball enthusiasts, historic Tiger Stadium in Detroit is just 20 minutes away by freeway. Photo by John Biever/Third Coast Stock Source

LEFT: The Detroit Pistons rule the world of pro basketball and draw sellout crowds to the beautiful Palace of Auburn Hills. Photo by Allen Einstein

to love, or at least tolerate, in July and August. The pools, at 19444 Lathers, 32929 Plymouth Road, and 9999 Harrison, open in mid-June and close at the end of August. Total pool attendance in 1989 increased to 24,674, with special days including Mother's Day, Father's Day, Kids' Day, and Grandparents' Day.

THE COLLEGES

Livonia is perfectly located when it comes to college athletics. If it's football you like, the University of Michigan is 35 minutes away in Ann Arbor and Michigan State is an hour up I-96 in East Lansing. Both are members of the Big Ten and both are perennial powerhouses.

Bo Schembechler is gone from Michigan, but other traditions continue. You need to buy tickets when they go on sale. Though the stadium seats 105,000 and is the largest such venue in North America, it has been sold out for more than two decades and, obviously, leads the nation in attendance.

Spartan Stadium in East Lansing seats 76,000 and sellouts aren't as routine. Though MSU doesn't enjoy quite as much popularity throughout the area as Michigan, and its teams haven't been quite so successful, the Spartans none-

theless have a tradition of contending for the Big Ten title and playing in post-season bowl games.

Both schools also boast excellent basketball programs, with MSU winning the NCAA title with Earvin (Magic) Johnson in 1979 and UM winning the NCAA title in 1989 under interim coach Steve Fisher.

Pssst. Here's a secret. If you love top-notch college football but don't like huge crowds or would like to save a few bucks, the Eastern Michigan Hurons in Ypsilanti are almost a well-kept secret. Tickets for the Hurons, annual contenders for the Mid-American Conference title, can often be bought on game Saturdays, and Ypsilanti is even a few minutes closer than Ann Arbor.

An even better-kept secret, though the football isn't quite as good, is the program at Wayne State downtown. A lot of Livonia-area kids who aren't quite good enough to play in Division I have played at Wayne State. Tickets are cheap and great seats on the 50-yard line can be bought on Saturday just before kickoff. Small crowds, huge bargain, good football.

And if its college hoops that gives you a thrill, there's no better facility in the Midwest, perhaps the U.S., than intimate Cobo Arena in downtown Detroit, where the Division I University of Detroit Titans play their games. The arena seats just 11,000 and the sight lines are superb. With the top ticket going for under $10 and the cheap seats for about $5, it's a bargain. And there are no bad seats in the house.

Eastern Michigan University also plays high quality basketball. Closer to home, the Schoolcraft College team features many local stars who play there for two years before heading on to scholarships at major universities.

Like hockey? Then, again, Livonia's the place to be. The University of Michigan has one of the finest hockey programs around, run by a former player, Red Berenson. After college, Berenson went on to a lengthy career in the National Hockey League, in the process opening up pro hockey to the college player. The finest players in Canada and the U.S. temporarily call Ann Arbor home, and many of them later play in the pros.

An even more successful program, under Ron Mason, is just a little farther up the road at Michigan State, where the Spartans had what could arguably be called the college team of the 1980s.

Where was the world record for attendance at a hockey game set? No, you'll never guess. It was at a college hockey tournament at Joe Louis Arena, home of the Red Wings in downtown Detroit, half an hour from Livonia. Each winter for the past 25 years, four college teams play a two-day tournament over the Christmas holidays. Though Joe Louis seats fewer than 20,000, more than 21,000 have filled every nook in the place for the college tournament.

And in the spring, Joe Louis is the site of the Central Collegiate Hockey Association playoffs, where such teams as Michigan, Michigan State, and Michigan Tech battle it out to see who will go to the NCAA tournament.

Each summer, some of the finest college baseball players in the U.S. call Livonia home. Six teams comprise the Livonia Collegiate League, which plays its games at Ford Field. A total of 96 players play 96 games over the course of the summer; many of the ballplayers go on to pro careers, and this is a chance to seem them close up.

THE PROS

There is no better atmosphere for professional sports than in the Detroit area. The Pistons built a new arena, the Palace of Auburn Hills, for the beginning of the 1988-1989 season; though it seats more than 21,000, they haven't had an unsold ticket since. The Red Wings hockey team plays in the biggest arena in the National Hockey League; the club routinely averages more than a sellout of 19,600, though standing-room tickets go for $14 apiece. Both clubs lead their leagues in attendance every year, though they often play their home games in conflict with each other.

The Tigers sell two million tickets a year if they're an average ball club. In 1989 they were horrible, and they still sold 1.7 million. Part of the reason is the incredible loyalty Tiger fans have for their team; some of it is that Tiger Stadium is just such an intimate, quaint, relic of a place to watch a ball game on a warm summer night.

The Lions football team has suffered through some tough years, but has returned to respectability and shows signs of possibly joining the upper echelon, thanks in large part to sensational running back Barry Sanders.

That's not the end of pro sports in the area. There's also a pro lacrosse team, the Turbos, and an indoor football team, the Drive, both of which play in Joe Louis Arena.

Last, but most certainly not least, is pro boxing. Detroit is home of Thomas (Hit Man) Hearns, and other recent world champions such as Milton McCrory and Hilmer Kenty. The world-famous Kronk boxing team, of which Hearns is the biggest star and which is run by Emanuel Stewart, is based here. Fight cards are abundant throughout the area, featuring both amateur and pro bouts, with regular cards at Cobo Arena and the Palace.

If you don't want to get out of the house after a day at work, but still love your sports, Livonia's got just the thing for you—cable televison. MetroVision, the local franchise, carries ESPN, which has sports 24 hours a day as part of the basic cable package. It also offers PASS, a premium channel that carries many of the Tiger, Red Wing, and Piston games, as well as college hockey and professional boxing.

THE INFRASTRUCTURE

andscaping can only do so much for a building. Sure, a pond out front is nice, as are flowering trees in the spring and some evergreens for winter. But all the landscaping in the world won't turn a bad building into a good one. The windows still need to fit tightly, the floors need to be level, and the infrastructure strong and impervious to rust.

Athletic events, symphonies, good restaurants, and nice places to shop are the landscaping of a city—all important but nearly irrelevant if the infrastructure is bad, if you can't get your garbage picked up on time, if the political infighting at City Hall immobilizes government, if the tax rate is too high, if the schools are bad, or if the roads are cracked and potholed.

Livonia's infrastructure is made of iron, bolted and welded together to withstand the winds and stresses of city life. "Livonia is the best-run city in America," says city assessor Ron Mardiros. And who's to say he is wrong? The city *is* well run. Its industrial corridor is a model for any growing city. Its millage rate is 60.15, one of the lowest in the state. Its schools actually educate. The roads are fixed in the spring, and salted on time in the winter. Politics is a tool of government, not its *raison d'etre*. Its older housing stock is well made and well kept. Its new subdivisions feature first class workmanship and details. In an era when entropy seems to have taken control of many city

Mayor Robert Bennett (right), who oversees what some call "the best- run city in America," attends a Memorial Day service in Veterans Park. The Michigan Stock Shop/ Steve Fecht

governments, Livonia works, and works better than it ever has.

CITY GOVERNMENT

Politics does not rule Livonia's city government.

That may not seem like much of a statement, but in the reality of local government, it says volumes. In some neighboring communities, politics is a combination rite of revenge, internecine warfare, and slapstick comedy that makes for wonderful headlines and lousy government.

Factions are swept in and out of office, charges of one kind or another fly back and forth, lawsuits are threatened or filed, bankruptcy is threatened or receivership filed—and readers of the local papers eagerly await the next chapter, especially in election years.

But not in Livonia.

Mayor Robert Bennett was elected to office in 1987. He replaced interim Mayor Robert McCann, who in turn had replaced Edward McNamara when he had been elected to the post of Wayne County executive. Bennett won an extremely spirited and close election with Joan Duggan, who was attempting to become the city's first woman mayor.

It was no secret that many officeholders in city government were active supporters of Duggan, including department heads. In neighboring cities, those that held non-civil service positions would have been out of a job on the new mayor's first day. In Livonia, the ax was never sharpened and no heads rolled. Bennett wasn't interested in revenge, or in putting cronies into high-paid government office. He was interested in good government, and Duggan's supporters happened to be good administrators; on their records, alone, they deserved to keep their jobs, and so they did.

It helped that Bennett was a former Air Force sergeant and manager at Michigan Bell who understood the benefits of efficient management. It helped, too, that Livonia in the past two decades had developed a tradition of good government at the expense of good politicking.

That wasn't always the case. In the 1960s, Livonia was a battleground between its strong-willed and overly argumentative mayor, Harvey Moelke, and a city council that seemed to be fighting vetoes on every vote.

Ironically, the animosity was good for the city; it united what had been a fractious council around a common dislike for the mayor's policies. Under the "strong council, strong mayor" form of government in Livonia, the council needs five votes out of seven to override a mayoral veto; under Moelke, the council began approaching its decisions with that five votes in mind. As a result, personal conflicts between council members were often put aside.

That spirit of consensus resulted in the current freeway system in Livonia—the council got together ahead of time, decided on an east-west route for I-96 and a north-south route for I-275, and presented it to a shocked Moelke as a *fait accompli*. The spirit of consensus also resulted in the formation of the Human Rights Commission—where McNamara, as a member of city council, feared Moelke was going to bring in vocal opponents and so made a phone call to Madonna College, which sent over 35 nuns to pack the front row at the city council meeting that gave birth to the commission.

It is that spirit of consensus that rules Livonia today. Reporters who come to Livonia after serving tours of duty in other suburbs are amazed at the level of cooperation at city council meetings, at the lack of grandstanding, at the lack of self-serving speeches in front of the cable TV cameras, and at how quickly and efficiently things are accomplished, for the most part with a minimum of tabling and a minimum of vote delays over tough issues.

Reporters are also pleasantly surprised by the open lines of communication they have with department heads and employees. Unlike in many cities, where press inquiries are directed through a public relations department or where comments can only come from the mayor, city manager, or one designated spokesman, Bennett, as did McNamara, gives the media full access. Employees and department heads are allowed—even encouraged—to return phone calls promptly and give honest answers, even to questions involving controversial issues.

Mayoral vetoes are used sparingly. Bennett doesn't use them as political tools—"See, I'm fighting for you, the voters"—but as a practical method for stopping a project he doesn't like. If Bennett knows a veto will be overridden, he allows the council's decision to stand. Why take up time, energy, and money beating a dead horse?

Enough praise for the system. Here's a quick guide to it:

CITY COUNCIL

The seven-member council approves budgets, sets tax levies, enacts local ordinances, approves lot splits and zoning variations, and approves contracts. It is made up of seven members who are elected at large. Every two years, four members are up for election; the top three vote-getters get four-year posts and the fourth gets a two-year term.

The council is part-time, meeting at night, with members usually holding down full-time jobs elsewhere.

The council holds study sessions every two weeks in the main auditorium, where issues are discussed. It holds voting meetings once in each of the other two weeks. In addition, the council has committee-of-the-whole meetings and other committee meetings in the council room on the sec-

ond floor of City Hall. All meetings, including committee meetings, are open to the public.

In January 1990, veteran council member Joan McCotter was voted by her colleagues to be council president, the first woman president in the city's 40 years.

ELECTED OFFICES

Elected offices in Livonia include, in addition to mayor and council, the posts of treasurer and city clerk. Both the treasurer's and the clerk's offices are on the first floor of City Hall.

The treasurer issues tax bills twice a year and collects payment for tax bills, water bills, weed cutting bills, and false alarm bills.

The clerk keeps records and documents pertaining to the city, issues and signs licenses, approves receipts and expenditures by the city, and administers oaths of office and elections.

DEPARTMENTS

Assessor The assessor assesses property and dispenses information about assessments, lot sizes, lot splits, legal descriptions, land ownership, and qualifications for filing for state exemptions.

Community Resources This department oversees the resident-resource program, which makes referrals for emergency food, clothing, shelter, and energy assistance; Livonia Youth Assistance, a juvenile delinquency diversion program for youths 7-16; the cable TV office, which produces government programming for Channel 8 and serves as liaison between the city and the private cable company, MetroVision; the seven city commissions (aging, arts, cable TV, historic preservations, historical, human relations, and youth); and senior citizen programs such as the two senior centers and free trans-

The tools of the fire trade await their use. The city's fire department does emergency medical runs as well as fire runs. The Michigan Stock Shop/ Steve Fecht

portation to banks, doctors and dentists, and shopping centers.

16th District Court Ordinance violations, small claims, traffic violations and misdemeanors are settled in district court, as well as arraignments for felonies, which are tried in the county's circuit court.

Engineering This department processes permits for work with public rights of way, inspects public construction work, reviews plans for public improvement, conducts engineering studies, and administers contracts. Under its aegis are street paving, sidewalks, streetlights, water and sewer location, and permits for soil erosion control.

Finance and Accounting Under the city charter, the finance department prepares

and administers the general budget, keeps accounting records, supervises purchases and expenditures, and oversees the complex investments that make money for the city. Millions of dollars are moved from account to account and bank to bank, often on a daily basis to take advantage of tiny changes in interest rates.

Fire Department The department handles firefighting, of course, as well as emergency medical service, with all fire fighters trained to do both jobs. About 85 firefighters provide 24-hour-a-day service from five locations. The budget for the department in fiscal year 1990 was $6.3 million, and, at 18 percent of the general fund budget, is the city's number two expense.

Housing Commission This commission oversees a wide range of public housing, rent subsidies, and loans for renovation and repair of private housing. There are three senior citizen apartment complexes—Brashear Towers, McNamara Towers, and Ziegler Place apartments—and one complex of stand-alone houses for seniors known as Silver Village.

Silver Village is just north of the sports and athletic complex, a scenic collection of buildings tucked into a forested setting. The village was so successful that in 1990 the city unveiled plans for a similar project on Newburgh Road between Plymouth and Grantland, scheduled for completion in the summer of 1991.

Inspection The department handles building and alteration permits, zoning compliance permits, and complaints regarding contractors, and enforces state and local codes.

Libraries Livonia has one of the best library systems of any city its size in the nation. The new Civic Center Library, adjacent to City Hall, is the jewel of the system. Opened in August 1988, the $8.5-million

ABOVE LEFT: The Melody
Men hit all the right notes
and provide great dance
music at the Senior
Citizens Center. Several
housing complexes, such
as the Brashear Towers,
McNamara Towers, and
Silver Village, cater to
seniors. The Michigan
Stock Shop/ Steve Fecht

ABOVE RIGHT: Church life
is central to the city, which
boasts about 65 churches
of all denominations and
sizes. Seen here is a service at St. Edith Church.
Photo by Gary Quesada/
Korab Ltd.

LEFT: The new Civic Cen-
ter Library is both visually
stunning and practical. Its
user-friendly computer service helps visitors find the
reading material they are
looking for. The Michigan
Stock Shop/Steve Fecht

library provides thousands of books; 16-mm films; video and audio cassettes; microfilms; and computerized search of area libraries for material not on the premises.

In addition to this state-of-the-art library, there are three branch libraries—the Alfred Nobel branch on Plymouth Road, the Carl Sandburg branch on Seven Mile, and the Vest Pocket branch on Farmington.

Ongoing programs at the various branches include children's programming, such as Christmas craft sessions, Snow-flake Story Hours, Battles of the Books, and seasonal contests; free noontime con-certs; senior-citizen services, including both hardback and paperback books with large print; and adult programming such as work-shops on improving energy use, financial planning, IRAs, and better gardening.

Parks and Recreation   This is one of the most active and utilized recreation depart-ments anywhere in a city this size. The city spends $3.2 million, fully 9.4 percent of its general fund budget, on parks and recreation.

Police Department   This is how highly Livonia's police department is thought of in Michigan: when a state-of-the-art com-puter system for identifying fingerprints was introduced in the state in late 1989, Livonia got one of just three systems in use by local police forces in the state (the State Police kept the fourth).

Eventually, more computer systems will be available. For the forseeable future, Livonia will give assistance on prints to po-lice in the nearby cities of Northville, Wayne, Westland, and Plymouth, and in the townships of Northville, Canton, Redford, Plymouth, Van Buren, and Sumpter.

Police Chief William Crayk—who, in a suit, looks more like a CEO than a cop who came up through the ranks—oversees a force of about 145 officers. As Livonia has grown, so have its police needs, and a major expansion of the police station was recently completed.

The department's 1990 budget is $11.8 million, about 34 percent of the city's general fund budget of $34.5 million. The police logs shows much of the crime restricted to malicious destruction of property, auto theft, and shoplifting. Crimes against people are much more infrequent—an armed robbery is considered a major, "hold-the-presses" crime by the *Livonia Observer.* There were no murders in 1988 and two in 1989.

Public Service   As the public service department goes, so goes the city. Everything else in the city can be run to perfection, but if the public service department was poorly run, everyone would suffer. Fortunately, it has a history of being well run and accessible by residents with problems. The department is responsible for maintenance of parks, roadways, water mains, and storm and sanitary sewers. It patches the potholes left after the tough Michigan winters, collects the leaves in the fall, puts salt on the roads and bridges in winter, trims trees in summer, helps residents with flooded basements, and runs the free woodchip program, the recycling center, and the city's household refuse site.

Sanitation   Residents have weekly curbside service. Service requires branches and yard rubbish properly bundled, and newspapers in bundles not to exceed 50 pounds. Large items such as old appliances are picked up upon request, at no extra charge. A recycling program was recently started, and has

exceeded expectations for participation.

THE PRIVATE SECTOR

A major portion of the infrastructure is, obviously, city owned or controlled. But much of it is run by other government units or is in the private sector.

Business   There are more than 3,500 businesses in Livonia, ranging from Mom-and-Pop party stores to the Ford Transmission plant on Plymouth, with its 4,000-plus employees.

Livonia has perhaps the best-organized industrial zone in Michigan. The hundreds of mostly light (and smokeless) industries in the zone make up nearly 16 percent of the city's tax base. Non-industrial commercial business accounts for 10.5 percent.

Scattered throughout the city, along the mile roads or the north-south main roads, are offices, medical and dental centers, strip centers, and shopping centers.

Some facts and figures:

—The largest employers are: Ford Transmission, 4,000 employees; Delco Products Division (GM), 2,500; Inland Fisher Guide Division, 2,000; Ford National Parts Distribution Center, 1,200; St. Mary Hospital, 1,175; Valassis Printing, 1,150; Buick-Oldsmobile-Cadillac Group, 900; Automobile Association of Michigan, 900; Foodland Distributing, 670; Awrey Bakery, Inc., 650; Michigan National Bank, 600; Madonna College, 500.

—Of all manufactured goods in Livonia, 73 percent are sold to customers in Michigan, with 17 percent for the balance of the Midwest, nearly 7 percent to the balance of the U.S., and just 3 percent for export.

—According to one survey, more than 77 percent of the businesses in Livonia have their corporate headquarters here; 52 percent also have locations outside Livonia.

—Livonia has a widely diversified industrial base. The percent of industry in the fabricated metals field is the largest, at 21 percent; only 3 percent were in the old standby of tool and die.

—There are 954 industrial businesses covering 2,151 acres; 726 businesses in 38 neighborhood business districts covering 345 acres; 594 businesses in 32 shopping centers or malls covering 376 acres; and 905 commercial or service businesses covering 852 acres.

—From 1988 to 1989, Livonia added 49 acres of commerical and office space and six acres of industrial space. It added 148 acres of residential land and lost 208 acres of vacant or agricultural land.

—Thirty-five percent of the businesses in Livonia have 10 or fewer employees; 85 percent have 100 or fewer.

—Fully 40 percent of Livonia companies rate the city as an excellent place to do business, and 53 percent rate it good. Only 4 percent thought it fair, 3 percent didn't answer the question, and, most significant, none said the city was a poor place to do business.

Chamber of Commerce   Livonia has one of the more active and growing chambers in the area. Membership for 1990 was about 1,200, up nearly 20 percent from 1,017 in 1984-1985.

With the dramatic influx of women into business and industry in the last 20 years, the "old boy network" no longer exists. A look at the chamber's roster of officers for 1990 confirms it—two of the four vice presidents are women, Marcia Buhl of Michigan Bell and Shirley Ritter of the Livonia Family YMCA. A check of the rest of the officers reveals the diversity of businesses from which they come—President Jack Kirksey, Livonia Public Schools; President-elect Tom Bjorklund, MetroVision Cable; vice president Ken Kelsey, Kelsey Advertising Specialties; and Richard Isham, Observer and Eccentric Newspapers.

The old boy network no longer exists, but networking is as strong and important as ever. The chamber facilitates networking, but also offers much more. It publishes a wide variety of publications, including a business and community directory, an industrial directory, a guide to starting a business, a regular newsletter, and a brochure of Livonia attractions.

The chamber opens up lines of communication between an individual businessperson and city, county, and state government; offers group insurance; has ties to political action groups for effective lobbying at the state level in Lansing; has a number of exclusive advertising vehicles; and can offer help with practical needs such as payroll services, site location, and expansion.

Churches   There are about 65 churches in Livonia, representing just about every faith and denomination.

Medical Facilities   St. Mary Hospital on Five Mile and Levan is a major facility in western Wayne County, with 304 beds. Run by the Felician Sisters, the hospital is one of several in the area that coordinate their emergency rooms to better handle incoming patients. After a massive accident during a heavy fog in 1989, for example, some ambulances were directed to St. Mary, others to Garden City Osteopathic.

St. Mary is also a major voice in the community. It is the city's fifth-largest employer, with 1,175 employees; it sponsors community events such as the Corporate Cup athletic competition each June; and it is the major beneficiary of the city's annual Heart Fund fund-raiser at the city's three municipal golf courses.

Scattered throughout the city are more than 260 doctors and medical clinics and more than 120 dentists and dentist offices.

Hospice service is available through Madonna College's Angela Hospice, which ministers to the needs of about 15 dying patients at any given time. "It's a way of

ABOVE LEFT: Schoolcraft College was ahead of its time, and proved to the naysayers the importance of a good community college. The Michigan Stock Shop/ Steve Fecht

ABOVE RIGHT: The presses roll at the Observer and Eccentric Newspapers, which publish 13 twice-a-week editions throughout metropolitan Detroit. Combined circulation is nearly 180,000, with the Livonia Observer *serving both as company flagship and as the city's official publication for legal ads and announcements. Photo by Gary Quesada/Korab Ltd.*

RIGHT: Madonna College boasts a new library for its more than 4,100 students. Photo by Gary Quesada/ Korab Ltd.

having patients die with dignity," says director Sister Giovanni.

Newspapers Two large dailies, the *Detroit Free Press* and *Detroit News,* provide national and international coverage. Local coverage is provided by the *Livonia Observer,* one of 13 suburban papers published twice a week by the Observer and Eccentric Newspapers, which are headquartered in Livonia at Levan and Schoolcraft. The O&E papers generally outsell the dailies in their readership area, which includes most of the affluent suburbs west and north of Detroit.

The O&E sells about 180,000 copies

Madonna College offers unique courses that are hard to find elsewhere, such as hospice care, Japanese studies, and a full-support program for the deaf. These sign-language students practice in an ideal setting on campus. Photo by Gary Quesada/Korab Ltd.

twice a week, with readership of about half a million. The *Livonia Observer* is the city's official newspaper and contains the city's legal ads and notices.

SCHOOLS

Public Schools Most of Livonia's residents are served by the Livonia Public Schools, which have 16,000 enrolled at one of the three high schools (Franklin, Stevenson, or Churchill) or the 23 elementary schools or four middle schools. A much smaller district, the Clarenceville Public Schools, serves residents in the northeast corner of the city as well as some residents in nearby Farmington Hills and Redford Township. There are 1,800 students in the two elementary, one middle, and one high school in the district.

The Livonia Public Schools operate adult programs at the Bentley Center, with about 2,000 adults availing themselves of various services at any given time. The district also operates vocational and handicapped programs for students from throughout western Wayne County.

Parochial Schools Ladywood High School, a Catholic high school, is located on Newburgh in the city, while a local boys high school, Catholic Central, is located in Redford, just a few miles from Livonia. There are two Catholic schools for kindergarten through eighth grade, and one for kindergarten through sixth grade.

There are two Lutheran schools for kindergarten through sixth grade.

Schoolcraft College When city fathers in the 1950s decided to set aside 183 acres of land for a community college, many residents thought they'd flipped their lids.

A community college? What's that? Those were two questions asked in an era before community colleges had found or defined their niche.

Other questions were: Why so much land? And why way out in the boonies, on Haggerty Road between Six Mile and Seven Mile at the extreme western edge of the city?

Thanks to the magic of hindsight, setting the land aside was one of the best things the politicians did since incorporating Livonia as a city in 1950.

Since Schoolcraft opened in 1964, more than 14,000 area residents have earned their two-year associate degree, more than 81,000 have transferred to four-year schools, and tens of thousands of others have taken non-degree courses to improve their job skills.

When Schoolcraft was built, the typical student was fresh out of high school. (The tax district for the school includes residents of school districts in Livonia, of course, as well as neighboring Garden City, Plymouth, Canton, and Northville townships, the city of Plymouth, and Novi.)

Today, there is no typical student. A recent study of 13,300 enrollees showed that 38 percent were under 22, with 42 percent age 22-34 and 20 percent over 34.

Only one-third of the students are in programs designed to lead to four-year degrees at other institutions. The rest are in career programs, from A (accounting) to W (welding and industrial fabrication) with stops at most of the letters in between (biomedical engineering technology, computer-aided drafting, criminal justice, laser-electro-optics, metallurgy, nursing, robotics, and small business management).

School officials long ago realized that there was a segment of the population that didn't fit into either a career-oriented program or a program leading to a four-year degree. That's where the school's ever-growing Continuing Education Services comes in, offering more than 250 classes, workshops, and seminars each semester, most of them stand-alone classes.

If you own a small business and want to learn how to computerize your operation, there's a class for you. If you're a nurse and want to brush up on the latest in infectious-disease control, there's a seminar for you. Maybe it's a lot of knowledge you need—you own a small machine shop and want to learn all the things you'll need to know to qualify for contracts with the Big Three car companies. Or maybe it's something a bit more basic—you've got a home computer but could use a few hours' instruction in mastering MS-DOS. Either way, Schoolcraft's the place to turn.

All that innovation in serving adults or businesses in the community doesn't mean that Schoolcraft has abandoned the traditional student. If college to you means the rah-rah of cheerleading and athletics, then welcome to Schoolcraft. In 1988, the school's women's soccer team won the National Junior College Athletic Association title and the next year the women's volleyball team won the NJCAA championship. The school also offers intercollegiate competition in women's and men's basketball, women's cross country, men's soccer, and co-ed golf.

Innovative course offerings have been a financial boon to the school, letting it use classrooms at night or on weekends when they might otherwise sit empty. That has in turn helped keep down the cost for students in traditional programs. In 1989, the resident tuition was only $33.50 per credit hour, among the cheapest in the state.

The school offers child care for kids 2½ to 6 at the main campus, and infant and toddler care at the smaller Radcliff campus in nearby Westland.

Madonna College   This private school at the northwest corner of Levan and Schoolcraft is one of the best-run in the nation, known for innovation in its course offerings. Its president, Sister Mary Francilene, was recently named by the Exxon Corporation as one of the top 100 college presidents in the country.

Defining the typical Madonna student is even more difficult than defining the typical Schoolcraft student. Though the school was founded by and is administered by the Felician Sisters, barely 50 percent of its student body is Catholic; while the average student age at Schoolcraft is 24, at Madonna it is 29. Madonna's record enrollment in 1990 of more than 4,100 was three-fourths female and nearly three-fourths part-time (with another 700 in noncredit continuing education programs).

The school prides itself on its liberal arts education, yet a major emphasis is on applied sciences and practical career preparation. If education in community and small colleges has evolved into defining niches and filling them, then Madonna has evolved more than most; people come here for classes they can't find elsewhere.

It is the only college or university in the state, for example, to offer a full-support program for the deaf, and offers other unique progams in church music, hospice

care, Japanese studies, nursing home administration, and emergency medical technology. Its programs may not be unique to the area, but are considered among the best—criminal justice, gerontology, and nursing, for example.

Unique? How's this? Madonna offers a Masters of Science program in administration in Taiwan; it beat out other schools in the state to win a contract from Michigan Bell to run a bachelor's program in business at on-site Bell locations; it sponsored a trade mission in Germany and England; and in the fall of 1989 it began its three-year sequence in Japanese language, history, and culture, the only program of its kind in metropolitan Detroit.

Though there is some natural competition for students between Madonna and Schoolcraft, there is also a close relationship between the two. Schoolcraft is Madonna's largest supplier of students for its 50 undergraduate and three graduate programs.

Though most of its students live off-campus, there are residential facilities for 250 men and women, who live in separate wings of one dorm. The school belongs to the National Association of Intercollegiate Athletics and offers varsity programs in men's and women's basketball, men's baseball and golf, and women's volleyball, softball, and tennis. Intramural sports include tennis, golf, basketball, flag football, floor hockey, and indoor soccer.

Service Organizations   Livonia is well served by an active body of service organizations, including the American Legion, Association of Retarded Citizens, Business and Professional Women, Jaycees, Kiwanis, Knights of Columbus, Rotary, Soroptimist, B'nai B'rith, and the Lions Club.

A CLIMATE FOR CULTURE

L ong gone, of course, are the days when Livonia was regarded as merely a suburb or a bedroom community. When the cities that surround Detroit were bedroom communities, residents usually had to drive into Detroit for their culture. That's where the plays were, that's where you found good restaurants, that's where you had to go to hear a jazz band or a symphony. No more.

Livonia's Arts Commission even has a telephone hotline today (425-2327) to keep residents abreast of the wide-ranging and constantly changing array of artistic endeavors going on in the community from month to month. Don't call unless you've got some spare time on your hands; it won't be a quick call, as there's a lot on the tape.

There might be news of:

—The Music Under the Stars concerts in the Civic Center Park, an annual, free series sponsored by the Parks and Recreation Department.

—The annual Livonia Public Schools Fine Arts Festival. The 14th annual festival in the spring of 1990 included jazz bands, pottery, jewelry making, paintings, drawings, and theater.

—The Aesop's fables production in progress at the Civic Center Library by the Churchill Advanced Theater Group.

—The wonderful noontime concerts at the library; one week it might be a solo flute performance, another week a trio on cello, violin, and piano. As always, they are

Francesco DiBlasi, the only director the Livonia Symphony Orchestra has had in its 18 years, conducts his troops at a Churchill High School performance. The Michigan Stock Shop/ Steve Fecht

free. Feel free to bring a brown-bag lunch.

—The Livonia Civic Chorus, which had its silver anniversary concert in May of 1990; or the Madonna College Chorale; or the Schoolcraft College Choir; or the latest Sweet Adelines concert; or the latest offering of the symphony orchestra.

LIVONIA SYMPHONY ORCHESTRA

In a time when cities of a million and more are struggling to keep their symphonies alive, Livonia's symphony orchestra keeps rolling along.

The orchestra began in 1973 as the Oakway Symphony, taking "Oak" from Oakland County and "way" from Wayne County. In 1988, symphony principals decided it would be better to drop the confusing "Oakway" name, which really meant very little to people in either Oakland or Wayne counties, and to base itself in Livonia.

Its director since its founding has been Francesco DiBlasi, a Livonian who was trained (on trumpet) at Juilliard and who has played with the New York City Opera, American Symphony Orchestra, Metropolitan Opera, and Detroit Symphony Orchestra. His conducting credits include the Grand Rapids Symphony, Scandinavian Symphony, Philadelphia Orchestra, Pittsburgh Symphony, Michigan Opera Company and Ballet Russe de Monte Carlo.

His 70 musicians are divided roughly into thirds: one-third are professional musicians who receive union scale; one-third are music teachers, who receive a more modest stipend; and one-third are promising students taking private lessons.

The result is a community treasure. The orchestra—or variations of it—plays nearly year-round in the city, including a music in the park series near City Hall. Its 1989-1990 season included a five-concert series at Churchill High School; a three-concert, Friday evening series at the Civic Center Library; a three-concert summer series; a six-concert chamber series; and its two tra-

ditional special concerts—"Merry Olde England Christmas Wassail" and the April "Cabaret." In addition, members of the orchestra can be found playing a benefit at Laurel Park Place or performing at the annual Heart Fund award night in December.

The symphony's repertoire is wide ranging and ambitious, from a night of French music and cancan dancing, to a salute to Gershwin, to a night of movie themes, to, of course, Mozart, Strauss, Debussy, Berlioz, Beethoven, and Bach.

The symphony gives more to the community than fine music. It is involved with an educational outreach program that coordinates projects with youth symphonies and other school-related programs such as the Center for Creative and Performing Arts in Livonia.

Artists don't find themselves alone in Livonia. They are generously supported by the Livonia Arts Commission, the Livonia Cultural League, the Arts Alliance Group, and the Michigan Council for the Arts; as well as the Livonia Chamber of Commerce, the Livonia teachers' union, and such governmental units as the city council and Livonia Public Schools.

CIVIC CENTER LIBRARY

Livonia has four libraries, but by far the pride and joy of the system is the new Civic Center Library just east of City Hall. A striking, three-story building that was opened in August 1988, the main library, which cost $8.5 million, is a state-of-the-art facility that is both user-friendly, thanks to its human help, and highly technological, thanks to its computerized card catalog, terminals, and microfilm system.

Branch libraries are the Vest Pocket Library on Farmington Road, the Alfred Nobel branch on Plymouth, and the Carl Sandburg branch on Seven Mile.

COMMUNITY THEATER

Southeastern Michigan is rich in community theater, and Livonia is no exception.

The fall of 1990 kicks off the 37th season of the Theatre Guild of Livonia and Redford (Redford is a neighboring township). Longevity is one trademark of the group; so too are first-rate productions and ambitious schedules.

The guild has its own playhouse, an intimate theatre in Redford. The group closed its 1989-1990 season with *Steel Magnolias,* a comedy/drama that requires a fine ensemble. Making the production doubly ambitious was the fact that the popular movie of the same name was out at the same time, and theatergoers carried their memories of the superb acting of the movie into the playhouse with them.

The 1990-1991 season kicked off with *The Belle of Amherst,* based on the life of American poet Emily Dickinson. The far-ranging season included a musical, a drama set in South Africa, and a comedy to close the season.

The fall of 1990 marked the beginning of the 10th season for Trinity House, a community theater group whose focus is non-mainstream, even obscure theater, much of it written locally.

In the 1989-1990 season, the group put on two long-running shows: one was a night of four one-act plays, and the other a full play titled *Junior High.* One of the one-

act plays and the full play, a musical, were written by Paul Patton, a Livonian.

The group, amateur in finances but not in the quality of production or writing, performs in the historic Union Church; the church's seating capacity of about 95 makes for wonderfully intimate theater and a true rapport between actors and audience.

Trinity House began as an offshoot of Trinity Baptist Church in Livonia, but organizers decided they wanted to focus more on theatricality than on proselytizing or preaching, and established independent status.

The 1990-1991 season calls for an expanded program of four shows.

COMEDY

Five nights a week, from Tuesday through Saturday, Livonians and their neighbors roar with laughter at Joey's Comedy Club on Plymouth, above Stoyan's Restaurant. The talent ranges from locals trying to make good to national headliners fresh from clubs in Los Angeles or New York.

Such is the level of the talent (and the decibel level of the laughs) that a production company filmed an HBO comedy special there in the summer of 1988.

One of the club's owners, Joey

The Livonia Symphony Orchestra used to roam through Oakland and Wayne counties as the Oakway Symphony. It now calls Livonia its permanent home. The Michigan Stock Shop/Steve Fecht

TOP: The new Civic Center Library, just east of City Hall, is impressive inside and out. This state-of-the-art facility is highly technological while remaining user-friendly. Photo by Ulrich Tutsch

Bielaska, even has his own cable TV show, *Spotlight on Comedy,* which features his headliners.

There are two shows on Friday and Saturday nights and single shows Tuesday through Thursday. Package deals are available for a show upstairs and dinner downstairs.

DINING

James Beard, the noted cook and food writer, once said that the Detroit area was his favorite restaurant place in the world, such was the diversity and quality of the ethnic fare in southeastern Michigan.

If some communities can be considered bedroom communities, perhaps Livonia should be considered a kitchen community. For one thing, there is the nationally renowned culinary arts program at Schoolcraft College, which has supplied extraordinary chefs to the world of gastronomy for a generation. For another, there is the astonishing range of restaurants in a city six miles square. The ethnic fare ranges from Japanese (Akasaka and Moy's Steak House) to Cantonese (Wing Yees) to Mexican (El Nibble Nook, home of what its regulars swear are the best margaritas in the world), to French (Le Bordeaux, where your meal comes with live music most nights) to Italian.

Livonia is perhaps best known for its wonderful collection of Italian restaurants. You'd think it was the, ahem, national pastatime.

Not only does Fonte D'Amore on Plymouth have an amazing assortment of pastas (fettucine alfredo with smoked salmon, farfalle gorgonzola, scallops pas-

Express yourself! This comedian and others do at Joey's Comedy Club. The Michigan Stock Shop/Steve Fecht

cara), but on Wednesday nights they are served up, believe it or not, with live opera.

Corsi's on Seven Mile is renowned for its northern Italian cuisine; DePalma's on Plymouth specializes in mouth-watering veal; Livonia Charley's on Schoolcraft caters to businesspeople at lunch and has a fettucine primavera that must be seen and tasted to be believed, replete with baby corn, red peppers, and Chinese peapods and smothered in cheese; and the Olive Garden, a national chain, is always crowded and always reliable.

The newest culinary center in the city is in or near Laurel Park Place in the northwest corner of the city. You could eat for months at the seven restaurants in the area and never have anything twice. Try the quiche, calimari, or grilled mahi-mahi at D. Dennison's Sea Food Tavern. Or the incomparable chili, fresh swordfish, or blackened chicken at Max & Erma's. Or the salmon filets at Garden Court. Or the quiche lorraine or orange roughy at Jacobson's. All of that and you haven't even left the mall.

Additional fare available at various places in Livonia includes two Detroit-area traditions: superb, messy, drippy Coney Island hot dogs, and hot, fresh pizza, either traditional or deep dish.

For those who want to combine their dining with a drive, Livonia is, again, centrally located. Windsor, half an hour east, is an eater's delight, with an incredible as-

sortment of ethnic food, much of it East Asian or Indian. For those who like it hot, there is an assortment of Thai restaurants. For those who merely like it wildly interesting, there are Vietnamese places.

And Ann Arbor to the west is also a haven for the culinary. Again, pasta is a specialty.

When it comes to the senses, whether it's hearing, seeing or tasting, Livonia's the place to get them treated.

NEIGHBORING AREAS

No city of 100,000 is going to claim a monopoly on culture, or even claim that it is fully representative of the cultural offerings of a certain geographical area.

Livonians are surrounded by a rich diversity of culture in southeastern Michigan.

ABOVE: Bates Hamburgers is a daytime and nighttime landmark. Its windowside stools look onto Farmington and Five Mile roads. The Michigan Stock Shop/Steve Fecht

FACING PAGE, BOTTOM: The storytime lunch hour always gathers together moms and kids outside the Carl Sandburg branch library on Seven Mile. The Michigan Stock Shop/ Steve Fecht

ABOVE: An art deco masterpiece, the Fox Theatre is now the largest-grossing theater in the U.S., hosting shows as divergent as classic movie revivals and concerts by top recording artists. Photo by Santa Fabio

ABOVE RIGHT: A restoration worker takes a break during the 1988 refurbishing of the fabulous Fox Theatre in downtown Detroit, less than a half-hour from Livonia. Photo by Santa Fabio

Just as Livonia serves as a geographic center for technology in southeastern Michigan, so too does it serve as a geographic center for culture. What cannot be found in the city can certainly be found to the east, north, south, or west.

Whether its an avant-garde piano performance at Hill Auditorium in Ann Arbor to the west, a rock concert at the Palace of Auburn Hills to the north, or an on-the-way-to-Broadway play at the Fisher Theatre in downtown Detroit, Livonians find themselves a short drive away.

Here is just a partial list of the cultural venues available to Livonians in their spare time:

Detroit Given its population of about one million, and its long history as a port town through which immigrants poured for generations, Detroit has a diversity of culture rarely matched in the world.

In one area of several blocks in downtown Detroit are no less than 10 theaters and the Detroit Institute of Arts. The magnificent Fox Theatre, an art deco palace recently renovated and restored to its original gaudy and beloved splendor, at a cost of millions, is currently the largest grossing theater in the United States, hosting shows as divergent as revivals of the movie *Lawrence of Arabia* and concerts by Frank Sinatra.

Touring acts from dance to jazz to reggae to classical can be found at the Music Hall Center for the Performing Arts, Masonic Temple, Fisher Theatre, State Theatre, and Orchestra Hall. Plays are performed regularly at the Fisher, the Hillberry Theatre, and the Bonstelle Theatre. The renovated Grand Circus Theatre will be the future home of the Michigan Opera Theatre.

Indoor Concerts Orchestra Hall in Detroit is known worldwide for its nearly perfect acoustics and is the site of chamber and classical shows, including regular performances by the Detroit Symphony Orchestra. Other Detroit venues include the intimate Music Hall Center, ornate

Masonic Temple, and spectacular Fox.

Touring rock bands and other acts requiring large seating capacities play in Detroit at Cobo Arena (10,000) or Joe Louis Arena (21,000).

Large suburban venues include the Palace of Auburn Hills (22,000) and the Pontiac Silverdome (76,000), both to the north of Livonia.

To the west of Livonia in Ann Arbor, Hill Auditorium, designed by Albert Kahn, has excellent acoustics and seating for 4,300. Nearby is the smaller Power Center for the Performing Arts.

Outdoor Concerts   Closest to home is the Concert in the Park Series at town center.

Burton Tower, Ann Arbor—The tower was designed by Albert Kahn and sits behind Hill Auditorium on the University of Michigan campus. Free half-hour carillon concerts are performed each weekday at noon when school is in session. Included are free trips to the top of the tower to watch the performer and catch a beautiful view of campus.

Chene Park, Detroit—A new, nine-acre park on the Detroit River, Chene Park is the scene of a wide range of free concerts, from rock to jazz to classical. Take a fishing pole and fish for coho salmon while you listen to the show.

Christ Church, Bloomfield Hills—Adjacent to the world-renowned Cranbrook Education Community, the church's 118-foot tower houses a 62-bell carillon that rings out an hour-long concert each Sunday in summer at 4 p.m. Feel free to sit on the grass outside the church.

General Motors Building, Detroit—All summer there is a wide variety of free concerts in the New Center area, across from the Albert Kahn-designed GM Building. Wednesdays from 11:30 a.m. to 1 p.m. and Thursday evenings from 5:30 to 8:30.

Hart Plaza, downtown Detroit—On summer weekends, a series of ethnic festivals

makes this a popular gathering spot for Detroiters and suburbanites. An amphitheater in the middle of the plaza is the site of weekly performances by various ethnic bands and musicians, as well as the site of the Downtown Hoedown each May, which is the world's largest free country music show, and the Montreux-Detroit Jazz Festival each Labor Day weekend. Most shows are free.

Huron-Clinton Metroparks—The parks are scattered throughout southeastern Michigan. The Detroit Symphony Orchestra plays a series of concerts in the parks each year. For information, call 1-800-24-PARKS.

Meadow Brook—This scenic outdoor concert site lies adjacent to a 100-room mansion on the campus of Oakland University to the north of Livonia, just northeast of Pontiac off I-75. This site has a smaller, more intimate, and friendlier ambience than Pine Knob.

Pine Knob, Clarkston—All the major and rock acts tour Pine Knob, a huge outdoor facility an hour north of Livonia along I-75. Pine Knob has thousands of covered seats in the amphitheater and thousands more on the surrounding lawn and hillsides, ideal for picnickers.

Down the street from the Fox, the Hillberry Theatre is a renowned part of Theater Row and a popular venue for Livonia's art and culture seekers. Courtesy, The Hillberry Theatre

2

LIVONIA'S ENTERPRISES

The area known as the Golden Corridor derives its name from the numerous burgeoning and architecturally dynamic commercial developments along I-275 on the western edge of the city. Photo by Balthazar Korab.

MANUFACTURING

Producing and distributing goods and foodstuffs, manufacturing firms provide employment for many Livonia area residents.

Photo by Ken Davies/Masterfile

ARGENT LIMITED

A t Argent Limited a dozen employees do it all—they research, invent, manufacture, and service the company's 150 different products for the metalworking industry. Argent's product lines include grinding coolants, cutting oils, drawing and stamping fluids, cleaning compounds, and rust preventatives. Using more than 250 basic ingredients in its products, the company specializes in solving specific problems for its customers, often inventing a new lubricant, coolant, or compound for the specific job at hand.

Argent Limited has earned an excellent reputation in the metalworking trade for its effective products, excellent service, and fair prices. The company's core of loyal customers in the aerospace, automotive, marine, machine tool, and agricultural implement industries continues to expand. "We do 90 percent of our business within a 250-mile radius of Livonia, although we have customers as far away as Florida and the West Coast," explains Lance Leonelli, president of Argent.

For 12 people to do everything from research to manufacturing, sales to service, each of Argent's chemists, chemical engineers, and mechanical engineers must wear many hats. This means customers are in direct contact with the people who make Argent products. Sharing responsibility has also led to a near-zero rate of employee turnover

since the company was founded.

Argent Limited is a classic story of a family-run enterprise. Since 1977, when the Leonelli family formed the company to purchase an existing operation at Brookfield and Capitol in Livonia, Argent's work force has tripled while sales volume increased more than eightfold.

In 1957 Bruno and Mollie Leonelli established the Aldoa Company in Detroit, which manufactures proprietary compounds and products for electroplating. Their son, Lance, worked in the business part time throughout high school and college, and then full time

(Left to right) Lance Leonelli, Bruno Leonelli, Mollie Leonelli, and Tony LaMarca.

after earning his degree. In 1977 the Leonellis bought the Tool & Abrasive Products Chemical Division of Ex-Cell-O Corp. in Dearborn, moved it to Livonia, and renamed it Argent Limited. They were the sole stockholders, and Lance became the president.

Meanwhile, Lance Leonelli's best friend since childhood, Tony LaMarca, had earned a degree in mechanical engineering, worked for Ford Motor Company, taught high school, and built racing car engines on the side. About one year after the Leonellis started Argent, Tony LaMarca came into the business, where he is now vice president/sales and service.

LaMarca sums up Argent Limited's plans for the future: "We plan to grow at a steady, manageable rate. Our main strengths lie in research and development and manufacturing, and we plan to expand our distributor network as we locate firms that share Argent's commitment to quality, service, and competence."

Argent Limited has earned an excellent reputation in the metalworking trade for its effective products, superior service, and fair prices.

GENERAL MOTORS—5 DIVISIONS

There is a lot of Livonia in a lot of GM cars and trucks. In fact, GM and Livonia go back four decades. Today more than 8,000 General Motors employees work at five important GM facilities in Livonia. They play a major role in building and servicing millions of GM vehicles nationwide. These five groups of the world's largest corporation have made a significant contribution to the economic life and growth of the city.

The General Motors Engine Division's Livonia Engine Plant on Middlebelt Road, just south of Interstate 96, currently builds engines exclusively for Cadillac cars, including the new Allante. Nearly 250,000 powerful V-8 engines are manufactured and assembled in the Livonia plant each year.

Since it opened in 1973 the plant has been widely recognized as a leader in innovative management concepts. Employee involvement, teamwork, and continuous improvement have been the hallmarks of the plant's operations. The result is engines that are among the best in the world for quality, reliability, durability, and performance.

The Inland Fisher Guide Division is one of the world's largest trim-manufacturing plants. In its 1.2-million-square-foot facility on Plymouth Road, approximately 2,000 employees make the interior trim for approximately 2.5 million cars each year. The trim produced at the Livonia plant goes into some of the cars under each major GM nameplate: Chevrolet, Pontiac, Oldsmobile, Buick, and Cadillac. In addition, the plant makes seats for selected GM models and vinyl tops for all GM automobiles.

GM's Delco Products Division on Eckles Road ranks as General Motors Corporation's largest nickel-chrome plating facility for bumpers. The plant also produces strut and spring assemblies for virtually all GM cars and trucks.

Originally built as a Chevrolet Motor Division plant in 1954, the facility has expanded steadily, along with the city of Livonia. In 1986 the plant became part of the Delco Products Division. Today more than 2,000 people work in the 2-million-square-foot plant to produce world-class components for GM and other automobile manufacturers.

The GM Service Parts Operation in Livonia supplies more than 550 GM car and truck dealerships in Michigan and northern Ohio with thousands of GM parts and accessories. The Service Parts Distribution Center has been doing business at its 250,000-square-foot plant on Schoolcraft Road since 1966.

The Publishing Services Activity of GM Photographic composes, prints, and publishes sales and service documents for all General Motors car and truck divisions. From its facilities in the Allied Commerce Center on Enterprise Drive, the Publishing Services unit generates materials ranging from ads to owners' guides and service related material for GM's car and truck divisions, advertising agencies, dealers, and customers.

There's a lot of Livonia in a lot of GM cars and trucks.

CONTRACTORS STEEL COMPANY

The impressive growth of Contractors Steel over the past three decades has been due as much to the firm's spirit of hard work and hustle as to its extensive inventory, custom processing, and rapid delivery.

In 1960 steel salesman Donald Simon saw the need for a local distributor who could rapidly supply steel items to Detroit contractors and decided to fill the gap. He rented the back of a lumber yard and a small office, bought a used truck, a mobile crane, and 25 tons of miscellaneous steel. Contractors Steel Company was in business, with Simon as president and principal crane operator, his wife as bookkeeper, and Mark Bokas as truck driver and loader.

From that modest beginning Con-

Contractors Steel Company's 14-acre, state-of-the-art steel service center complex includes a 110,000-square-foot warehouse, three crane yards, a 100,000-square-foot plate storage area, and the company's office building.

tractors Steel grew into the thriving firm that today turns over more than $60 million per year, employs 150 people at three plants, and serves 5,000 customers in eight states. Its inventory of 55,000 tons of prime steel includes 3,500 different items, making Contractors one of the most diversified steel distributors in the Midwest.

The company provides prices on all inquiries within an hour, picks and processes the steel, and can ship it the same day. Although beams and plates are the biggest sellers, the company stocks everything from steel rounds weighing two pounds apiece to 30,000-pound one-foot-thick steel plates. Items can be punched, sheared, bent, flame-cut, or sawed according to customer specifications.

"Attitude is everything," says Simon, explaining his company's success in a fairly flat market. "Every one of our employees has to be a hard worker, ambitious, and dedicated. We've got a large, diversified stock and can do a variety of first-step processing. But

OPPOSITE: Quick access to the steel products is a key to prompt customer service. With this five-ton capacity "order picker" Contractors Steel Company has the ability to immediately store and retrieve items from their 1,400 pocket rack storage system, which holds over 5,500 tons of steel.

that's just the start—we offer very competitive pricing, the fastest loading and shipping in the business, and a motivated sales team." According to general manager Mark Bokas, the firm's three branches get up to 300 orders from the approximately 400 inquiries they receive each day.

Contractors Steel moved its headquarters from Detroit to the new community of Livonia in 1968, and its 110,000-square-foot warehouse is located on a 14-acre site on Amrhein Road. In 1975 a second warehouse was opened in Wyoming, Michigan, near Grand Rapids, and in 1986 this plant was completely modernized and expanded. In that year the company opened a third facility in Twinsburg, Ohio, 18 miles south of Cleveland.

In the Livonia plant today 14 overhead cranes, a 30-ton lift truck, and two depressed bays operate day and night to quickly load the orders. The firm's 25 tractor trailers then deliver items from the three Contractors Steel locations to customers in the Midwest and the East.

Contractors Steel marked its 30th anniversary having proved that it is possible to survive and even thrive in a difficult marketplace. The enterprising spirit that Simon, Bokas, and several of their children have brought to the company has firmly established Contractors Steel Company as a major steel distributor in the Midwest, with excellent prospects for continued growth.

LTV MISSILES AND ELECTRONICS GROUP
AM GENERAL DIVISION

S ince 1984 Livonia has played a part in the remarkable history of AM General, a leading producer of military vehicles in the Free World. The company's history goes back to the turn of the century and the early days of the automobile and encompasses the development of the universally-recognized jeep during World War II and hundreds of thousands of postal vehicles, buses, and a variety of military trucks.

In 1903 the Standard Wheel Company of Terre Haute, Indiana, a bicycle manufacturer, decided to branch out into "horseless carriages." The company set up the Overland Automotive Division, which manufactured the "Runabout" model. In 1907 John Willys, then a car salesman, bought out the company. Under Willys' leadership, the company known as Willys-Overland thrived. In 1915 Willys was the country's second-largest automobile manufacturer.

By 1940, as war approached, Willys-Overland designed America's first four-wheel-drive, 1/4-ton, general purpose utility vehicle ("general purpose" was shortened to "g.p." and became "jeep"). More than 350,000 jeeps rolled off the assembly lines during the 1940s, and the GIs' beloved vehicle remained popular in peacetime as well.

During the Korean conflict Willys-Overland designed an improved utility truck, the M38, and produced over 150,000 of them. In 1953 the company

The M1 Abrams tank, surrounded by proud and dedicated AM General employees.

was purchased by Henry J. Kaiser (of Kaiser-Fraser), and as Willys Motors until 1963 then as the Kaiser Jeep Corporation it produced civilian passenger cars and tens of thousands of delivery vehicles for the postal service during the next two decades.

In 1964 Kaiser Jeep bought the former Studebaker Chippewa Avenue plant in South Bend, Indiana, and went on to win many contracts to manufacture Army trucks and postal vehicles.

American Motors bought Kaiser Jeep in 1970, and soon the Defense and Government Products Division became the AM General Corporation, a wholly-owned subsidiary of American Motors Corporation. The 1970s held many successes for AM General, including the development of three different series of military trucks. The company patented the central tire inflation system, which allows the driver to change tire pressure to suit a particular terrain while the truck continues moving.

AM General's largest and most recent success began in 1979. In a

highly competitive situation the division began "from scratch" design work on the M998 series—the High Mobility Multipurpose Wheeled Vehicle (HMMWV) also known as the "Hummer." In 1981 the U.S. Army awarded AM General a contract to develop a prototype of this 1-1/4-ton truck. Test results were excellent, and in 1983 the firm won the competition for a $1.2-billion, 5-year contract to produce 55,000 Hummers.

In the same year, LTV Corporation purchased AM General from American Motors and in 1984 moved the product engineering and research group into the present 220,000-square-foot facility in Livonia. AM General is now the vehicle manufacturing unit of the LTV Missiles and Electronics Group which also produces missiles, rockets, space systems, electronics, and avionics. Today, 400 permanent and contract employees in Livonia provide engineering and technical services to support many military vehicles, including the Hummer, the M9 Armored Combat Earthmover (ACE), and the M1 Abrams tank. AM General headquarters are located in South Bend, Indiana, and the company also has two manufacturing and service plants in Indiana, as well as an office in Washington, D.C.

Now on its ninth decade of manufacturing vehicles, AM General has established a worldwide reputation for quality products and services for government clients.

AM General employees, proud of the "Hummer" contribution to our armed forces.

EMBEST, INC., A DIVISION OF COUNTRY FRESH

Embest (short for Eastern Michigan's Best) is a division of the Country Fresh Corporation, which produces and distributes dairy products throughout Michigan. In its Livonia plant Embest manufactures a full line of Country Fresh milk and ice-cream products for customers in the eastern part of the state. The Embest division also supplies private-brand products to supermarkets and regional distributors.

In 1982 Country Fresh, the Grand Rapids-based producer and distributor of dairy products, brought in Delton Parks as its new president and general manager. Under Parks' leadership the corporation made a major commitment to expand its markets in eastern Michigan. To achieve this, Country Fresh reactivated and updated the vacant Delcrest dairy plant in Livonia, a facility in which Parks had worked some years before. Originally built by Allied Foods to serve the Wrigley supermarket chain, the plant began to be renovated in

March 1982 and was completed in less than three months.

In addition to the Embest, Inc., division, which accounts for 25 percent of the company's sales, the corporation's largest facility, the G.R. Best plant in Grand Rapids, produces a diverse product line that includes milk, ice cream, water, ice, orange juice, cottage cheese, yogurt, sour cream, and dips. In 1986 Country Fresh acquired the McDonald Dairy Company of Flint, with branches in Alpena, Battle Creek, and

Established as the eastern Michigan branch of Country Fresh dairy products in 1982, Embest, Inc., has since expanded its Allied Commerce Center plant, improved processing and material handling, and developed healthier and better-tasting products.

Traverse City. Country Fresh's smaller Frostbite division in Clare, Michigan, manufactures ice-cream novelty products that are sold under different labels throughout the state.

CORVO IRON WORKS, INC.

Detroit's Riverfront Towers and Cobo Hall expansion, Southfield's Prudential Town Center, and Novi's Civic Center all have one thing in common: steel fabricated by the Corvo Iron Works.

In business since 1968, Corvo has become one of the largest structural steel fabricators in Michigan. The company buys steel from mills and warehouses and fabricates it by using highly skilled workers and automated equipment. Corvo primarily takes on large construction jobs for corporations and manufacturers, such as Ford Motor Co. in Livonia, and various renovations, additions, and repair projects throughout southeastern Michigan.

Corvo's 65,000-square-foot structural steel plant is located on a 25-acre site in Novi, where steel beams and columns for major construction projects are made. In the 35,000-square-foot plant on West 8 Mile Road in Livonia, workers skillfully fabricate iron items such as staircases and handrails which

ABOVE: Corvo and Midwest Steel Erection constructed the Ford conveyor trestle over one weekend without interfering with scheduled commercial train traffic.

LEFT: Over 5,300 tons of Corvo structural steel went into the Prudential Town Center in Southfield.

have been incorporated into such diverse structures as Joe Louis Arena and Oakland Community College. Corvo also maintains field crews to erect and install custom-fabricated items on customers' sites.

Corvo's annual sales exceed $18 million, and the company employs 100 to 150 workers. "From the initial detail-

ing on many different engineering designs through fabrication and erection—and facing many tight time schedules—Corvo project managers work one-on-one with the client. We always work to meet the highest quality standards," according to Joseph A. Broad, president of the Corvo corporation since 1985.

HUGHES ELECTRONICS PRODUCTS CORP.

A 1982 headline might have read, "Satisfied Customer Buys Hughes Electronics." Richard Smith had been working as a project engineer for a local firm, designing circuit boards and often coming to Hughes Electronics Products to get them manufactured.

"One day over lunch David Hughes mentioned that he wanted to sell the business. Five months later, Carol and I were the new owners," Smith recalls. They kept the Hughes name because the company had established an excellent reputation for manufacturing printed electronic circuit boards and doing electronic assembly.

"We wanted to keep all the best features of the company, such as giving personalized attention to every customer and helping to design boards that would be more economical to produce. That open and friendly atmosphere, along with highest quality work, has led to a lot of repeat business over the years," Smith says. "And we definitely have found our niche in small-run projects."

On the other hand, the new owners

immediately began to update and modernize the plant. Since 1982 they have replaced 90 percent of the equipment, including drilling and routing machines, and installed all new photographic equipment. The result has been a remarkable increase in productivity of the company's stable number of employees and greatly improved efficiency in almost all phases of production.

In its attractive 7,200-square-foot facility at 34467 Industrial Road, Hughes Electronics' in-house capabilities currently include circuit boards, silk-screen printing, assembling, wave soldering, cabling and harnessing, final assembly, and testing. The firm earned UL recognition for board manufacture in 1989.

The company's varied client base ranges from "mom-and-pop" businesses to the largest automotive companies, from start-up computer firms to large utilities and several university research units. Its typical customer is a local division of a national corporation with a problem that demands a special solution.

Many of the special boards made at Hughes Electronics are used in automotive test equipment, remote control units for overhead cranes and material handling equipment, and computer interfacing. A surprising number go into

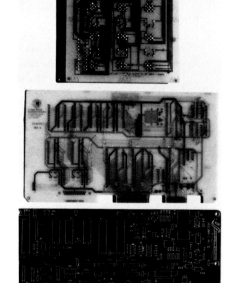

This photo shows the contrast between an old-style circuit board (top) and a new-style circuit board (bottom) produced by Hughes. The new board is 12 inches long.

controls for model planes and railroads—to run up to 16 trains at once. "We see a lot of people working out new products. It's an exciting business," Smith notes.

The firm's business comes mainly from southeastern Michigan, but it extends to many other states as companies move or when satisfied customers change jobs. Today Hughes-made boards are operating on four continents.

The company is currently setting up a separate facility nearby to expand assembly operations, and in 1990 the firm began in-house manufacture of multilayer printed circuit boards. A $40,000 wastewater treatment system has also been added recently. And, in the future, the company plans to do surface mount assembly work as volume expands.

A final factor in the success of this Livonia firm is family involvement. A University of Michigan economics graduate, Smith's wife, Carol, has worked full time in the accounting, purchasing, and scheduling side of the business for many years.

Hughes makes boards in a variety of shapes and sizes. This circular board is five inches in diameter.

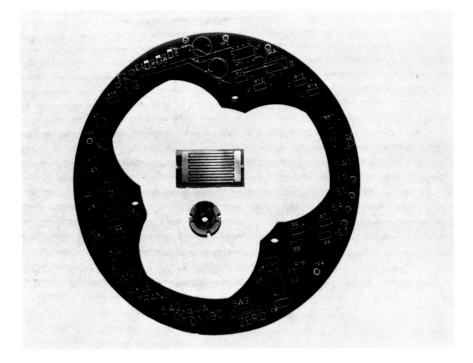

DETROIT BALL BEARING

Small bearings, huge bearings 27 feet in diameter that cost $250,000 ... bearings for chairs, hinges, mixers, cars, steel mills ... the world moves on bearings. Since 1920 Detroit Ball Bearing has grown to be the largest bearing distributor in Michigan—and the fourth-largest in the United States.

Today the firm has 29 service centers, most of them in Michigan, and the Livonia service warehouse is one of the company's largest. When the Livonia branch opened in 1955, antifriction bearings were still the principal product. As industry in and around Livonia grew over the years, the service center moved into new and larger quarters at 30984 Industrial Road in 1975, always adjusting its inventory to meet local needs.

In addition to standard bearings, Detroit Ball Bearing now provides power transmission products; electric motors; material-handling equipment; hoses, fittings, and assemblies; V-belts and rubber products; O-rings and retaining rings; adhesives, sealants, and lubricants; and much more. Through a mainframe computer network, the Livonia Service Center has access to the master warehouse stock of more than 160,000 items from hundreds of major manufacturers.

Computers also link DBB directly to many customers for rapid ordering and unmatched service. The Livonia center takes pride in having requested items in stock over 90 percent of the time. The company pioneered "just-in-time" inventorying in 1979, and leads the field in adapting to customers' systems.

According to District Manager Hil Gross, "The bottom line is customer service. When customers call, day or

One of Detroit Ball Bearing's largest service centers, the Livonia warehouse customizes its stock to meet customers' needs 24 hours a day, every day.

night, we have to deliver those parts quickly to keep their business going."

MAURER-SHUMAKER, INC.

On almost every GM, Ford, or Chrysler car today, a careful observer can find Maurer-Shumaker chemicals on one or more of its nuts and bolts or other fasteners. From its plant at 37025 Industrial Road off Newburgh, this small but fast-growing firm manufactures industrial chemicals, including cleaners, oils, coatings, and phosphates (zinc, iron, and manganese) for many large and small metal-treating companies that supply the auto industry, including Masco Corporation, the Cold Heading Company, Federal Mogul, and many others.

Founded in 1978 by two seasoned chemists, Terry Maurer, president of the company, and Gary Shumaker, vice president, the firm employs other experienced chemists in product development, manufacturing, and service. Maurer-Shumaker is regarded as a specialist in heavy zinc phosphates, although the firm manufactures a broad range of products including cleaners for steel; various phosphate coatings; organic coatings such as paint, pigmented oils, and primers, which are all applied over phosphates; and oils that inhibit corrosion. One or all of these products can be applied on small metal fasteners that go into cars, appliances, and buildings.

Today the market for metal fasteners demands finishes that are more corrosion resistant, nontoxic, and reliable than ever before. Because of size and experience, Maurer-Shumaker can move quickly to develop new products and get them into the market.

"One reason our business is growing is that we try to out-service our competitors," Terry Maurer says. That commitment to service, together with on-time delivery, fair prices, and high-quality products, add up to an unbeatable combination.

Maurer-Shumaker, Inc., serves the

Maurer-Shumaker's employees and distributors. Back row (from left): G. Shumaker, C. Cosner, J. Thompson, E. Knebel, A. Benoit, D. Stanton, and R. Barach. Front row (from left): D. Singelyn, G. Torcolletti, B. Ifkovits, S. Choren, and T. Maurer.

U.S. and international metal-finishing market through its manufacturing centers in Livonia; Toronto, Canada; and Toulouse, France, with several other licenses under negotiation. The company has also established an extensive network of North American and European distributors and a sales force of more than 30 engineers who promote and service Maurer-Shumaker chemicals around the world.

HYGRADE FOOD PRODUCTS CORPORATION

Whether they call them frankfurters or wieners or hot dogs, Americans eat 1.2 billion of them each year at ball games, backyard barbeques, and meal times. The Hygrade Food Product's plant in Livonia has been turning out an increasingly large market share of franks, as well as bacon, hams, and luncheon meats, since it was built in 1968.

Today the 95,000-square-foot facility at 38200 Plymouth Road is one of four Hygrade meat processing plants. Livonia is best known for Ball Park franks, although it also makes Hygrade hot dogs and variety meats, West Virginia bacon and hams, and Grillmaster chicken franks.

For a long time Ball Park franks were mostly popular in the Detroit area. In 1957 they were chosen as the official hot dogs for Tiger Stadium, and during a regular season Tiger fans now eat between 1.5 and 1.8 million of them. The 2.5 million hot dogs that were consumed in the stadium during the 1984 pennant year came close to the all-time record of 3 million.

Over the past 20 years Hygrade began an intensive national marketing campaign for Ball Park franks and other products. The result was that by 1980 they were distributed nationwide, and today Ball Park is the second-largest-selling brand of hot dogs in the country—and working hard to be number one.

Each week 1.5 million pounds of meat product come out of the Livonia Plant. Frankfurters account for about one million pounds, while about 150,000 pounds each of bacon and luncheon meat are shipped to stores and supermarkets from Montana to Key West, from Houston to Syracuse.

Hygrade acquired Grillmaster brand in 1976. In 1976 they introduced Grillmaster chicken franks, which are made from fresh rather than frozen chicken. Over the past 20 years Americans have been eating two or three times more poultry franks than before, and today about one-sixth of the company's franks are made from chicken.

Hygrade's Livonia plant also processes premium quality West Virginia brand bacon and hams that reach a particular market niche. Before each major holiday, ham sales gradually increase to one million pounds per week.

The history of Hygrade Food Products goes back to 1914, and includes many purchases and mergers in the United States and overseas. As of spring 1989 Hygrade became a subsidiary of Sara Lee.

In 1982 an unfortunate hoax cost Hygrade Food Products more than one million dollars. Ball Park franks had to be recalled because razorblades had supposedly been found in a couple of packages. On the positive side, the city of Livonia rallied support under banners such as "Livonia Loves Hygrade," and local residents consumed nearly 150,000 Ball Park franks. Thanks to fair-minded U.S. consumers, the company recouped its losses within one year. As Livonia residents proved after the 1982 hoax, Livonia appreciates Ball Park franks—and Hygrade Food Products Corporation.

More than 1.5 million pounds of franks and other meat products are processed each week at Hygrade's Livonia plant.

TECHNICOLOR VIDEOCASSETTE OF MICHIGAN

Who would guess that Livonia is the videocassette capital of the world? Nearly a quarter of all videocassettes for America's videocassette recorders are duplicated and packaged at Technicolor Videocassette of Michigan. The firm's Livonia plant is the largest single videocassette production facility in the world, and its sister facility in California is the third largest.

Set back from West 7 Mile Road near Interstate 275 on 24 acres of wooded land, this enterprising company in a booming industry was turning out more than 150,000 cassettes per day by the end of 1989. By August 1990 this grew to nearly 300,000 per day—sometimes running seven days a week—to feed America's insatiable appetite for home entertainment. The market keeps growing—more than 96 percent of U.S. households have color televison, and about 70 percent of those households have VCRs.

Technicolor Videocassette in Livonia obtains exclusive contracts with many of the top Hollywood-based movie companies to reproduce their films onto millions of high-quality videocassettes.

In modern buildings designed specifically for this purpose, truckloads of blank tapes and cassette boxes are transformed into VCR movies. Duplicating huge quantities of tapes involves hitech control rooms, environmentally controlled clean rooms, and thousands of VCRs continuously copying films.

The facility, built in 1986, is an architectural delight designed to fit into its natural setting. Offices look out onto woods, ponds, and wildlife, as does the three-story-high window of the employees' cafeteria. This building has been the site of several civic functions and charity benefits.

In 1987 this former division of CBS/Fox Video, Inc., was acquired by Technicolor, Inc., a holding company with two divisions: Technicolor Film and Technicolor Videocassette. The latter

Nearly a quarter of all prerecorded videocassettes for America's videocassette recorders are duplicated and packaged at Technicolor Videocassette of Michigan. The firm's Livonia plant is the largest videocassette production facility in the world.

has branches in California, the United Kingdom, Holland, and Livonia.

When people rent or buy a videocassette, there is a good chance that it was processed in Livonia at Technicolor Videocassette of Michigan.

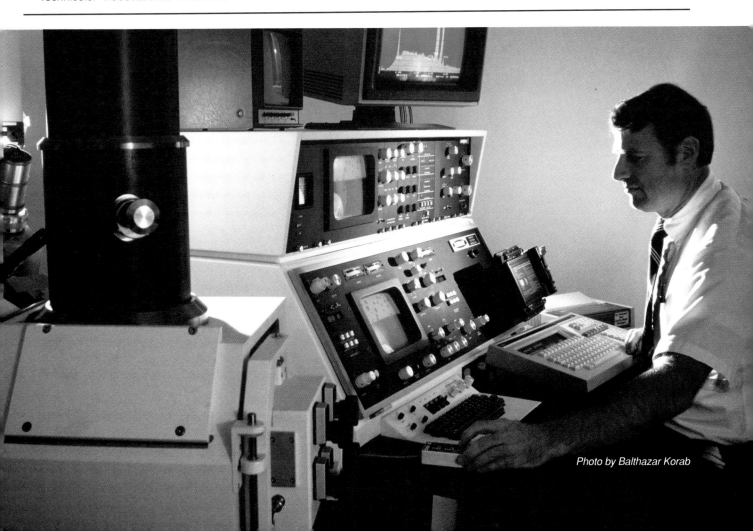

Photo by Balthazar Korab

MARKETPLACE

Livonia's retail establishments, service industries, and accommodations are enjoyed by residents and visitors alike.

Photo by Gary Quesada/Korab Ltd.

LIVONIA MALL

One thousand silver dollars were given away every day to shoppers during the week of October 23-29, 1989, to celebrate the silver anniversary of Livonia Mall. After more than 25 years of successful operation, the mall has grown from 40 stores to more than 90, and several major additions and renovations have helped to maintain its position as a popular and up-to-date shopping center for area residents. The most remarkable feature of Livonia Mall, however, is its commitment to the community—every day, every year, since 1964.

Livonia Mall was developed by two men of vision who became business partners more than 30 years ago. Jack Shenkman, an insulation contractor and land developer, and George R. Klein, a residential builder, not only envisioned Livonia's progressive future, but also worked hard over the years to make it a reality. They had the foresight to anticipate that shopping centers would be the wave of the future in retailing, and that enclosed, climate-controlled malls would take the lead.

Shenkman and Klein purchased a large parcel of farmland near 7 Mile and Middlebelt roads in the early 1960s, and began their pioneering development of the first enclosed mall in the metropolitan Detroit area.

When it opened for business in October 1964, the 625,000-square-foot, climate-controlled mall's 40 retail stores were anchored by Sears, Crowleys, and, for many years, a large Kresge store.

Both Klein and Shenkman were actively involved in the development and management of Livonia Mall through the years, and Mrs. Klein continues to work with Shenkman since her husband's death in 1988. Jeanne Hildebrandt, who has been the general manager of Livonia Mall for 17 years, started out as a bookkeeper soon after the mall opened and learned all aspects of operations as she progressed to her current position.

"Managing Livonia Mall is like running a city within a city," Hildebrandt says. "Day to day, all systems have to function—maintenance, accounting, secretarial, leasing, security, advertising, and more. Livonia Mall employs about 50 people to make sure the mall runs smoothly—and that doesn't include the people who work for the merchants."

The mall now houses close to 90 retail tenants in approximately one million square feet of enclosed space. In addition, the shopping center features six restaurants, a multi-screen movie theater, and customer services including medical and dental practices, a weight loss clinic, a shoe repair service, and a photo processing unit.

"Part of our job is planning for the future, so that Livonia Mall will continue to

meet the needs of a broad spectrum of Livonia consumers, in an environment that all age groups find enjoyable and comfortable. This means carefully balancing the retail mix, and expanding and renovating the mall to stay ahead in a competitive market," Hildebrandt explains.

In October 1987 a second Grand Opening celebrated the addition of a new wing to house 16 new merchants, plus a large Mervyn's store, which has joined Sears and Crowley's as an anchor of the mall. At the same time that

With more interior garden space and increased open access to stores, the Livonia Mall is more pleasant and beautiful than ever.

Sears completed a major remodeling of its store in the Livonia Mall in 1985, and it now carries more diversified name-brand merchandise than ever.

the new wing was built, the entire mall was renovated and updated from stem to stern, including lowered ceilings, tiled floors, oasis areas, more open and inviting store entrances, and many redesigned interiors for the mall's established stores.

In keeping with its aim of remaining a premier family shopping center, Livonia Mall will add a new Children's Palace store in 1990, offering an added attraction for young families with children.

Livonia Mall's management also provides "good neighbor" services, which include opening the mall early each morning for a year-round walking program, offering free classic movies once a week, sponsoring concerts by big name bands of the '50s and '60s, carrying shoppers' packages out to their cars, and making sure that senior citi-

Crowley's has been one of two principal anchors of the Livonia Mall since 1964. Constantly upgraded merchandise lines and a magnificent renovation have affirmed the Crowley Milner Co. store as a major attraction for Livonia shoppers.

zens who live near the mall get home safely.

In addition to caring about patrons' comfort and safety, Livonia Mall has enjoyed excellent relations with the city and has been a member of the chamber of commerce since it opened for business more than 25 years ago. Jack Shenkman, George Klein, and Jeanne Hildebrandt have each participated in numerous local government, civic, and charitable activities, including serving as members on the chamber board, the city's Planning and Industrial Development Commissions, the President's

Cabinet of Madonna College, and the Foundation Board of Schoolcraft College.

Livonia Mall has also contributed funds as well as facilities to many worthwhile charitable causes, such as hosting the annual Chamber of Commerce Harvest Ball. In February 1989 the mall sponsored a gala dinner and a concert featuring Tony Bennett to benefit the Michigan Cancer Foundation. The proceeds went entirely to charity, as they have after many other mall-sponsored fund-raisers, including benefits for abused children, the Livonia Family "Y," and a children's hospital, to name a few. Even coins tossed into the mall fountains go to charity. On a personal level, Mr. Shenkman has been very generous over the years in contributing both his time and resources to local charities as well as to political and religious groups in the southeastern Michigan area.

In the future Livonia Mall management will remain devoted to keeping its "city within a city" thriving—and continuing to work closely with the City of Livonia, the chamber of commerce, and with civic and charitable groups. Jeanne Hildebrandt sums it up this way: "Livonia Mall's future is as a partner with the community. That's why we've always given our total support to ensuring that Livonia remains a great place to live and work."

FOODLAND DISTRIBUTORS

Foodland Distributors is Michigan's largest voluntary food wholesaler. Its distinctive delivery trucks—white with a prominent blue and yellow "F"—are a familiar sight on Michigan highways. From the company's headquarters in Livonia, Foodland's fleet of 70 diesel tractors and more than 250 trailers travel as far north as Saginaw and as far west as Battle Creek, supplying more than 170 supermarkets with a complete range of food and household goods. Most customers of Foodland average two or three deliveries per week, while some larger markets require daily deliveries.

Motorists on Middlebelt Road, just south of I-96, can easily see Foodland Distributors' one-million-square-foot warehousing complex. The 83,000-square-foot freezer warehouse is bigger than two football fields and is the largest one of its kind in Michigan.

Founded in 1984, Foodland Distributors now employs more than 750 people. The company has been achieving an annual sales volume well exceeding $700 million on its stock of more than 22,000 items. The firm warehouses an extensive range of name-brand products, plus a complete line of Nature's Best and Home Best private label items.

Foodland Distributors, which acquired Abner Wolf's wholesale company in 1990, is now able to offer its customers very competitive prices due

Foodland Distributors' distinctive delivery truck.

Foodland Distributors supplies groceries, produce, meat, seafood, household goods, health and beauty aids, and an extensive line of delicatessen and bakery products to more than 170 Michigan supermarkets.

to its size and buying power. This relatively young wholesale distribution company serves Kroger stores and other chain and independent supermarkets in Michigan, including many that have Foodland in their names.

Foodland Distributors takes pride in being one of the most well-rounded wholesalers in the supermarket business. In addition to its large line of food products, the company offers its customers a wide range of retail support services, including pricing programs, centralized billing, shelf management, and advertising and promotional services. Foodland offers a variety of training programs for supermarket employees, including instruction in areas as diverse as creating party trays and detecting shoplifters.

Entering the 1990s Foodland Distributors plans to further expand its customer base while continuing to offer all customers a total spectrum of products and support services.

"We've been very successful," says Gregory F. Gallus, company president. "Our client base is growing, and so is the number of services we provide to our customers. We look forward to many more happy, productive, successful years serving independent and chain supermarkets in Michigan."

WONDERLAND MALL

Wonderland Mall has the honor of being the oldest and the largest shopping center in Livonia. Today the mall offers area residents approximately 120 stores, services, and eating places under one roof. Dominating the southwest corner of Plymouth and Middlebelt roads, Wonderland was opened in 1959 as an open-air mall and immediately became a landmark in Livonia. In 1983 it was purchased and exclusively managed by Schostak Brothers & Co., Inc. Renovation of the mall was begun in 1986 to enclose, completely renovate, and expand the mall to nearly one million square feet of retail space.

Wonderland Mall started with the best, like Montgomery Ward on the eastern end and A.J. Foland & Co. on the northwest, and fused them together with exciting new attractions, including Dunhams and Gantos Boutique, offering incredible values. The most recent addition came in 1989 when a 102,000-square-foot Target store and six-screen

AMC theater were added to the complex. Currently, the shopping center is in another phase of expansion to keep pace with the preferences of Livonia shoppers.

To complement the merchandise offered by the department stores, many Wonderland Mall shops specialize in women's, men's, and children's apparel, jewelry, shoes, toys, notions, and novelty items. Numerous other tenants offer a wide range of convenient customer services.

Not only can Wonderland Mall fill the complete shopping needs of the entire family—its array of restaurants, food shops, and theaters make it an entertainment destination as well. In the Eaton Place Food Court located in the north side of the mall, the hungry shopper or movie-goer has a choice of more than 11 eating places that offer everything from subs to salads, tacos to

The Wonderland Mall allows shoppers to take advantage of approximately 120 stores, services, and eating places in a beautiful and relaxing atmosphere.

'taters. In addition to the food court, the mall's restaurants include Cosmopolis Cafe, Coney Island, Little Caesars Pizza Station, Olga's Kitchen, Woolworth's, and Elais Brothers Big Boy.

As a major retail presence in Livonia, Wonderland Mall continually adapts the changing consumer needs. It plans to expand its already unmatched number and variety of merchants to keep pace with the area's growth in the 1990s.

HOLIDAY INN-LIVONIA

One of Livonia's first hotels, the 150-room Holiday Inn at 30375 Plymouth Road continues to offer excellent value with extensive amenities to business representatives, families, and leisure travelers.

Personal attention and outstanding staff are the keynote. General Manager Patrick Campbell worked full-time at the desk 10 years ago before training in many Holiday Inns around the country, then brought his experience back home.

"Our staff of 65 full- and part-time employees make all the difference" Campbell says. "Dona Burns has been a desk clerk since the late 1970s, and knows everyone. The housekeeping staff is outstanding. We have meeting rooms, up-to-date sleeping rooms, and fine food and drink."

The guest list now includes business clients, many tour groups, and families that return to this corporately owned and operated hotel for an excellent

package of amenities, including Piper's Restaurant with its country atmosphere and daily specials, Plum's Lounge, featuring large-screen TV and video music on weekends, and an outdoor pool. A short walk away are Wonderland Mall, the Ladbroke racecourse, the Terrace Theatre, and more.

The hotel's king leisure rooms and standard double rooms have been expanded and redecorated. All rooms feature work areas, cable TV and movies, coffeemakers, and room service. Dry cleaning, laundry, and 24-hour FAX services are also available.

For business groups, clubs, and social occasions, the Plymouth Road Holiday Inn can furnish the banquet rooms, good food and drink, and per-

Piper's Restaurant offers home-style cooking in a comfortable country atmosphere.

sonal service that bring guests back again and again.

CHARISMA SALONS

When hairstylist Richard Asztalos opened his first beauty salon more than 25 years ago, he was 19, and at that time Livonia had more farms than office buildings. Comparing his first salon to the beautifully modern Charisma Salon in the Laurel Park

Charisma Salons are designed for comfort and beauty to give customers the ultimate experience in pampered luxury.

Place shopping complex, Asztalos says there are few similarities—except that people still love to be pampered.

Asztalos' dream of providing the ultimate in luxury for clients who want to stay healthy and look good has come true at Charisma. Clients can be whisked away by limousine for a full day of beauty treatments including a manicure, pedicure, facial, massage, hairstyle, and lunch, finishing with a makeup session to complete the new look. "Businesspeople are under tremendous pressure today, and they need a release," Asztalos says. "You have to give something back to yourself, and after a day with us, you're ready to take on the world."

Charisma caters to both men and women, with the salon discreetly organized with one side for women and another for men. The full-service salon has a staff of 38 professionals offering the most up-to-date techniques in all aspects of care for hair, skin, nails, and

massage. In keeping with its emphasis on service, Charisma is open seven days a week for clients' convenience. Gifts called "Looking Good Grams" are an excellent way to offer beauty services to friends and relatives, and company employee incentives are available.

A lecturer at national and international beauty seminars, Asztalos is recognized for his involvement in professional education. Charisma offers fashion shows for groups, clubs, and businesses within the community to show off the latest trends. He has also produced videos on hair cutting and styling. Recently, he purchased a California-based company that manufactures botanical beauty products, called Concentrics, with distribution in over 2,000 salons nationally.

Another Charisma is located on 8 Mile and Middlefelt, also in Livonia, and features many of the same services and quality products that make people look good and feel great.

LAUREL PARK PLACE

Laurel Park Place—the elegant new retail, office, and hotel complex at 6 Mile and Newburgh roads—has become a major attraction for shoppers and business visitors to Livonia. Imposing archways, domed skylights, and marble floors create an elegant architectural setting for more than 60 stores and services, with the largest Jacobson's store ever built as the centerpiece.

Located next to the I-275 freeway and close to the Chicago-Detroit Interstate 94, Laurel Park Place is easy to reach from Detroit, Ann Arbor, Farmington, Bloomfield, Canton, and many other nearby cities. For year-round comfort climate-controlled passageways link the beautiful new 225-room Marriott Hotel and convention center, three atrium office buildings, a 10-screen movie theater, and the upscale retail mall. Enclosed and surface parking lots accommodate up to 3,500 vehicles.

Joining Jacobson's are more than 60

other retail stores, including Gantos, Eddie Bauer, Jos. A. Bank Clothiers, Williams-Sonoma, Gap Kids, and more. There are also several imaginative restaurants where shoppers can enjoy a beverage or a meal.

Developed and managed by Schostak Brothers & Co., Inc., of Southfield, Laurel Park Place officially opened

in November 1989, and has hosted many community events ever since that time.

With its distinctive atmosphere, accessible location, and exciting blend of shopping, restaurant, hotel, and office facilities, Laurel Park Place enhances Livonia's appeal as a city that is growing in attractive, innovative directions.

N. LEONE & SONS, INC.

The name itself tells people that N. Leone & Sons is a family business, and the history of this family-run food-service distribution company goes back more than 70 years. Nunzio Leone arrived at Ellis Island from Italy in 1909, and in 1922 he moved to Detroit, where he operated a grocery store at different locations on the city's east side for many years.

After World War II Nunzio's sons Ralph and Armando helped out in the grocery business. American GIs in Europe had been exposed to foods from different countries, and after they came back, they began to look for restaurants that served ethnic cuisine, especially Italian. Leone's grocery store began to supply more and more products to these restaurants—and started offering the now-traditional Leone 100 percent guarantee on every item sold.

By 1955 Nunzio and his son Armando reorganized N. Leone & Sons into a food-service distribution company, specializing in supplying establishments that provide food directly to the public. The company operated out of Detroit until 1962, when it moved to Livonia to get closer to the growing markets in Detroit's western suburbs. The Leones bought the former Sibley Lumber Company property on Plymouth Road between Merriman and Middlebelt for their wholesale facility. Ralph rejoined his brother, Armando,

N. Leone & Sons specializes in rapid delivery and individualized service.

and his father that same year. In 1976 Armando's son, Joe, joined the company after he graduated from college. Joe became president of N. Leone & Sons in 1986.

Today Leone & Sons is a full-line food distributor that sells to family restaurants, schools, hospitals, universities, government facilities, in-plant food services, caterers, hotels, specialty delicatessens, and fast-food restaurants. Leone's fleet of 25 trucks and trailers delivers food products throughout Michigan, northwest Ohio, and northern Indiana.

From stocking about 50 items in the 1950s, the company has increased its current product line to 6,500 items, including dry groceries, dairy products,

N. Leone & Sons stocks about 6,500 items in its 150,000-square-foot warehouse.

frozen foods, meats, produce, cleaning supplies, paper products, beverages, and restaurant supplies and equipment. More than 120 employees are needed to supply Leone's 2,000 customers on schedules ranging from a weekly to a daily basis.

Because most of their customers are short of storage space, the Leone company specializes in just-in-time inventory management and rapid delivery. The N. Leone & Sons warehouse contains almost 150,000 square feet of combined dry, freezer, and cooler storage space. Workers process 40,000 cases of products each week, most of them ordered today for tomorrow's delivery.

"Our company can immediately respond to changing tastes and to demands for new carry-out or ready-to-serve products," Joe Leone explains. "Just as important, customers know that they can get immediate, individualized service when they call us."

Joe Leone currently serves as vice chairman of the board of EMCO, an organization of more than 120 independent U.S. food-service distributors; he will become chairman of the EMCO board of directors in 1991.

A.R. KRAMER COMPANY

With one of the largest single-unit floor covering stores in the United States, the A.R. Kramer Co. in Livonia also covers a lot of ground when it comes to quality and customer service. The company's spacious retail store on Middlebelt Road near Five Mile Road offers a total line of floor covering, from wood to carpeting to vinyl to area rugs.

Kramer's has established such an excellent reputation that the Livonia firm covers all the floors in all Ford Motor Company buildings in North America, plus many at the University of Michigan and Detroit's Renaissance Center.

A family-owned business, the company was founded in Detroit by the first A.R. Kramer in 1925. Originally a door-to-door salesman, Kramer weathered the Depression with great difficulty, and afterwards gradually rebuilt his business with the help of a contract to carpet all Michigan State Police posts.

Kramer's son, the second A.R.

(Alan), came into the business in 1953. Under his leadership the firm moved to its current Livonia location in 1971. A major expansion in 1974 brought the facility up to 28,000 square feet of retail and warehouse space.

Since 1986, when his father retired, the third A.R. (Arthur) Kramer and his brother Michael have become the owners of the company, acting as president and vice-president. The firm has won many large local contracts such as the Livonia Civic Library and the Court House, and continues to put an emphasis on quality and customer satisfaction.

The A.R. Kramer Co. credits its 120 employees for the top-quality custom installation and client-centered service that has been responsible for the success of the company. As Art Kramer says, "We're competitive with the big chains in terms of price for quality, but we give our customers better service than they can get anywhere else"—and today that goes beyond Michigan.

PROFESSIONAL FOOD-SERVICE MANAGEMENT, INC.

Although many Livonia residents may not be familiar with the company, the financial division of Professional Food-Service Management at 15449 Middlebelt Road helps to put Livonia on the map. P.F.M. has branch offices and food service contracts at more than 100 locations in 35 states.

The firm's accounting division takes care of the payroll and benefits for more than 5,000 employees across the country and is also responsible for the purchase of and payment for thousands of food items from 2,500 vendors. In terms of incoming and outgoing mail, P.F.M. is the 10th-largest user of postal services in Livonia.

Founded in 1965 by Lawrence A. Pande, Jr., and his partner (now retired), the company celebrates 25 years of growth in 1990. Although corporate headquarters are located in Illinois, P.F.M. financial offices have always been in Livonia, under the direction of Earl Falk, Jr., executive vice

president and chief financial officer.

"P.F.M. provides custom food services for about 90 colleges, many summer camps, and several large corporations," says president Pande. "At one of our largest sites, Southwest Texas State, 500 to 600 of our employees operate dozens of food service units—including dormitory cafeterias, snack bars, vending machines, pizza delivery, football training tables, and even faculty receptions."

The company's recipe for success includes adapting to the needs and tastes of its customers. P.F.M. aims at providing food that is economical, using only the freshest and highest quality ingredients, preparing the food carefully, and serving with a smile. As Larry Pande likes to say, "Our food is better than others' and as good as mother's."

P.F.M.'s decentralized and participative organization gives managers the independence to innovate and tailor-make each particular location. Traditionally, the chief beneficiaries of a successful company are its owners. P.F.M., however, offers its employees the golden opportunity to benefit from their company's success by giving them a beneficial interest in it through their Employee Stock Ownership Plan. Falk notes that "30 percent of the company is now employee-owned. And as P.F.M. grows, so will each employee share."

Photo by Balthazar Korab

PROFESSIONAL LIVONIA

A n active and various amalgamation of businesspeople and professionals assures Livonia's growth into the future.

Photo by Balthazar Korab

LIVONIA CHAMBER OF COMMERCE

Its backbone is a fast-growing industrial corridor. Its heart lies in the pleasant, well-kept houses and spacious suburban yards. Its schools are among Michigan's best. Its chamber of commerce is among the state's 10 largest and possibly one of the most active in support of its 1,200 members. That's the city of Livonia, and as its chamber says in videos, on radio, and on T-shirts, "It's a Good Life."

The corridor south of Interstate 96 includes more than one thousand industrial, high-technology, service,

wholesale, and retail businesses, with many more located elsewhere in the city. Combine this with extensive residential areas, parks, first-rate city services, three major malls, many other

shopping centers, its position in relation to Detroit—and people generally agree that Livonia is a fine city.

According to John W. White, executive director of the Livonia Chamber of Commerce, the 25-year-old chamber has gone out and asked Livonia businesses what they want—what they need to survive and prosper.

About two-thirds of the members have fewer than 25 employees in their businesses, and about half employ 10 or less. There is a strong tradition toward family-owned and -managed companies, low employee turnover, and hard work.

The Livonia Chamber of Commerce is very active

The Livonia Chamber of Commerce has guaranteed a "good life" for its members. Both the chamber headquarters building and the organization's concept of what a chamber can do for its members has grown since it first began a quarter-century ago.

on behalf of its members and on behalf of the city. It promotes networking and professional contacts, offers business assistance services, supports member businesses through exclusive advertising and promotional opportunities, and expresses the viewpoint of Livonia businesses to city, county, and state governments.

"Businesses that join the chamber get added credibility," White says. "Members who get involved in our committees get an insider's perspective on community development, business and economic development, and government procedures, while they have a chance to pursue issues that are important to their own businesses."

The chamber has done much to bring the Livonia business community together and define its identity. It sponsors a year-round program of legislative and speaker luncheons, Five O'Clock Business Connections, an annual business exposition, and a number of social and fund-raising events.

Held each May, the Greater Livonia Business Expo has been a sellout since its inception four years ago. In 1990 the event was renamed Expo 275, to indicate that exhibitors from 10 other communities near Interstate 275 were taking part. More than 130 exhibitors and more than 5,000 attendees participated in the three-day event, including an opening night reception for 1,200 people.

"Expo's real benefit is in helping each business reach its market and get face-to-face with its best prospects," says Mike Cooney, director of economic development and retention for the chamber and show coordinator. "One new mailing business told me they wrote more orders during this year's show than they had during the whole previous year."

Other chamber services give businesses the tools they need to grow. These free or low-cost services include

access to its mailing list, site-selection guidance, business information and statistical analysis, and seasoned advice from the Business Development Team. Addressing two of the most basic needs of small businesses, the chamber offers an attractive insurance package for all chamber members.

First among the chamber's many publications is its pocket-sized brochure, *Livonia: Discover the Variety*, describing the attractions and key features of the city. Also widely used is the chamber-sponsored *Livonia Business and Community Directory*, sent free to every business and household in the city. The chamber also compiles a list of all businesses in the industrial corridor south of I-96 in the *Livonia Industrial and Related Business Directory*, which lists companies alphabetically and by service or product.

The Communicator, the Livonia Chamber's 28-page monthly magazine, is recognized as the best chamber of commerce publication in southeastern Michigan. It too is an advertising vehicle open only to member businesses. And for those new to business or new to the area, the chamber's guide, *Starting Your Business in Livonia*, gives

a head start on success.

The chamber-sponsored Greeter Service welcomes residents who move to Livonia from another city with a personal visit by a greeter and a coupon book of free or discounted goods and services. More than 50 chamber members currently use this exclusive advertising service to help them stand out from the 4,700-plus businesses in Livonia.

In conjunction with the Livonia Mall, the chamber sponsors an open-invitation Harvest Ball, featuring first-class entertainment and exciting prizes.

John White, a manager with Consumers' Power for 28 years, has served as the Livonia Chamber of Commerce executive director since 1984. Under his leadership, membership and the activities sponsored by the organization have both continued to grow. City Planner John Nagy expresses the view shared by many in city government that the relationship between the city and the chamber is excellent. "It's a working relationship based on mutual support and compatible goals," says Nagy. "We work well together—and that benefits the businesses in our community and the community as a whole."

More than 5,000 business people attended the three-day Expo 275, which celebrated an economic alliance among Livonia and 10 other communities located near Interstate 275.

STEVENS DESIGN SERVICE

S tevens Design Service in Livonia designs special machines, sheet metal dies, fixtures, and gauges for the automotive and aircraft industries.

Computer-aided design (CAD) systems help Stevens Design Service ensure quality, efficiency, and dependability.

Stevens has designed fixtures for the hull of the XMI tank, machines to produce parts for turbine aircraft engines, and dies for manufacturing all automobile parts—from wheels to bumpers, doors to roofs.

The firm began business 25 years ago, and its first major account was Chevrolet's Livonia division (now Delco Products). At that time Stevens' eight employees did all the design work by hand. Today, in a more spacious facility at Industrial and Stark roads near Interstate 96, 35 employees do manual work and use computer-aided design (CAD) systems to produce designs for companies such as GM, Ford, Chrysler, General Electric, and the Budd Company.

Stevens' CAD work stations can in-

terpret clients' data and specifications on its system, produce three-dimensional imaging of surfaces, and design tool-cutter paths that tool and die companies use to manufacture the designed parts. To stay competitive in the market, Stevens Design Service continually updates its computer capabilities.

Just as important, the success of an engineering design business such as Stevens' depends on quality, efficiency, and dependability. Mark Stevens, the firm's vice president, says, "We hire good people, and then give them any additional training they need to do the job."

Kirk Stevens, president of Stevens Design Service, says: "This company has been built on teamwork; we work as a team, and everyone has a voice. Maybe that's why most employees stay with the company once they start. That longevity is a big factor in keeping our quality and efficiency high."

KAMP-DiCOMO ASSOCIATES

K amp-DiComo Associates was founded in 1971 by architects Ervin E. Kamp, AIA, and Donald A. DiComo, AIA, who previously worked together in a Detroit-area architectural practice. Their extensive experience in commercial, industrial, medical, municipal, and educational design is reflected in the variety of projects the firm takes on.

An emphasis on complete design/build services, from site planning through construction, led the firm to form an affiliated company specializing in construction management, KDA/CM Incorporated, in 1974. "We combine our more than 50 years of experience and knowledge of all the major building trades and subcontractors with a design that has built-in flexibility," explains Donald DiComo, who has served as the firm's construction project manager since 1984. "This allows us to complete our projects on schedule."

"Putting the design on paper is one

thing—but it takes experience to get your design built as drawn," DiComo says. "We're bringing back the tradition of the architect as master builder." Currently, KDA builds nearly two-thirds of the buildings it designs.

In addition to architectural design and construction management, Kamp-DiComo offers construction, site planning, architectural, mechanical, electrical, and structural engineering, interior design, and administration of construction contracts.

Locally the firm has been awarded major projects by Madonna College and the City of Livonia, including the Civic Center Library. Other major projects include the Interstate 96 Officenter, Quality Inns in Livonia and Romulus, the Laurel Manor Conference Center, and renovations to the clubhouse at Northville Downs. The firm also man-

Civic Center Library—Livonia, Michigan

aged construction for the renovations of downtown Northville.

Kamp-DiComo Associates also designed its own headquarters on Middlebelt Road. "We serve clients throughout southeastern Michigan, but there's still a lot of growth that keeps us very busy quite close to home," says Ervin Kamp. "We design buildings that we're proud of—buildings that add to the many things this community has to offer."

SCHOSTAK BROTHERS & CO., INC.

M ost Livonia residents are familiar with the name of Schostak Brothers & Co., Inc. The company owns and manages Wonderland Mall and the new Laurel Park Place Shopping Center and Office Complex, as well as the K mart shopping plaza at 7 Mile and Farmington roads. Many other properties in the area, including the Manufacturers Bank Operations Center at 6 Mile and Haggerty roads, have also been developed and managed by this enterprising firm with corporate headquarters located in nearby Southfield.

Since the 1920s three generations of Schostaks have established a real estate leadership tradition. The firm was founded by Louis H. Schostak, and presently includes his son, Jerome L. Schostak, president and CEO, and his three grandsons, Robert, David, and Mark Schostak, currently all vice presidents. With a staff of more than 500 people, Schostak Brothers & Co., Inc.,

ABOVE & LEFT: Schostak Brothers & Co., Inc., developed and now manages many of the most familiar Livonia-area buildings, including the new Laurel Park Place shopping center and office complex.

BELOW: The First Center Office Plaza in Southfield is another Schostak Brothers project.

today is the largest full-service commercial real estate company in Michigan.

The firm has extensive experience in the fields of real estate development, brokerage, and property management, with particular expertise in shopping center management and development. In fact, Schostak Brothers now ranks among the top 25 companies in shopping center acquisition and development in the nation.

In addition to the three successful shopping centers in Livonia, the company has developed the Alpena Mall, Cherryland Mall in Traverse City, Macomb Mall in Roseville, Universal Mall in Warren, Shelby Corners in Utica, and more than 25 K mart retail developments, as well as other enclosed and strip malls in Michigan and Indiana.

From the inception of a development to its completion, Schostak Brothers

emphasizes teamwork between financial sources, partners, and architectural and construction agents. This principle of teamwork extends into the careful integration of leasing marketing, and management activities which assure the success of the development.

Schostak Brothers' experience enables the company to combine the

right mix of local, regional, and national tenants to create a successful enterprise. The firm's reputation has attracted such national "blue chip" retailers as Jacobson's, Sears, J.C. Penney, Dayton-Hudson, and K mart to these centers.

Schostak Brothers and Co., Inc., has achieved and continued to build its rep-

utation as an outstanding, productive, and visionary force in real estate—in development, management, brokerage, and also in retailing. Area residents can expect to see and use more Schostak shopping centers, office complexes, and multi-family developments in the future.

PARSONS & BOUWKAMP

T he law firm of Parsons & Bouwkamp, P.C., specializes in workers' compensation and general liability litigation, serving some of the nation's largest insurance companies, risk management organizations, health care systems, and businesses.

The principals of Parsons & Bouwkamp bring highly specialized experience and a client-centered approach to the defense of workers' compensation claims. This focus gives the firm a depth of knowledge and ex-

The professionals at Parsons & Bouwkamp bring highly specialized experience and a personalized, client-centered approach to the defense of workers' compensation and general liability litigation claims.

pertise usually found only in the largest law firms. At the same time, Parsons & Bouwkamp offers the individual service and personal contact possible in a smaller legal practice.

Each of the principal attorneys has extensive litigation experience and is personally involved in managing client

relationships and individual case litigation. Gary D. Parsons graduated from the Detroit College of Law with honors and was a law clerk for the Michigan Court of Appeals before entering private practice. Parsons is a member of the State Bar of Michigan, and both he and Bouwkamp are admitted to practice in the eastern and western U.S. Federal District Courts, the U.S. Court of Appeals of the Sixth Circuit, and the Michigan Supreme Court.

Stephen C. Bouwkamp earned his

juris doctorate cum laude from the Detroit College of Law and was a law clerk for the U.S. District Court before joining in practice with Parsons. Both partners are members of the Livonia Bar Association and are licensed to practice in the states of Florida and Hawaii as well as Michigan. The firm also has offices in Venice, Florida.

The firm's other associates include Roy R. Winn, Michael J. Pendracki, and Marsha J. Ellison. Winn, a 1975 graduate of the Detroit College of Law, specializes in general liability matters, including intentional tort, automobile no-

fault insurance, subrogation, wrongful discharge, and discrimination.

Michael J. Pendracki, a 1985 graduate of the Detroit College of Law, works primarily with cases involving general civil litigation, including divorce, collection, contract disputes, and property damage. After receiving her law degree from the Wayne State University School of Law, Marsha J. Ellison joined Parsons & Bouwkamp to specialize in appellate and general civic litigation.

"In the past decade, the costs of workers' compensation claims have risen dramatically, so that employers were forced to take a more aggressive stance in defense of these claims," says Gary Parsons. "Workers' compensation and other personnel-related cases such as wrongful discharge and discrimination often involve extensive research to mount an effective defense. In addition, litigation can extend for months or even years with potentially large settlements against employers. That's why our specialized expertise is so important. We emphasize early fact finding and preparation for trial or resolution."

Among the firm's clients are Allstate Insurance Company and Cincinnati Insurance Co. as well as the self-insured administrators, the Michigan Hospital Association, Penn General Services, Insurance Management services, Cranbrook, Corporate Services, Alexis, Inc., and Consolidated Risk Management. Through the auspices of these companies, Parsons & Bouwkamp represents employers in nearly every industry in Michigan. They currently handle workers' compensation claims throughout southeastern Michigan, from Muskegon and St. Joseph to Port Huron and Mount Clemens, including the major business centers of Detroit, Flint, Grand Rapids, and Lansing.

PROCTOR HOMER WARREN, INC.

Our mission is to serve our clients. For over 100 years Proctor Homer Warren, Inc., has been providing individual and business clients with the highest-quality insurance and real estate services," states Woods Proctor, chairman of the board of the Troy-based firm. To give this personalized insurance service to clients in the Livonia area, PHW recently opened a branch office at 32788 Five Mile Road, between Mayfield and Brookfield.

"We offer a broad range of services, reflecting our ability to handle all aspects of insurance," states Tania Auton, senior vice president. "Because we are independent agents representing many of the leading companies, PHW can tailor insurance programs to clients' needs and pocketbooks, and at the same time provide fast and reliable claim service."

While most of PHW's commercial insurance is handled by experts in the firm's Troy headquarters, the Livonia agency specializes in a full range of home, vacation property, automobile, life, and disability insurance. Aircraft and marine coverage, accident and health insurance, estate planning and income protection, and special art and antiques coverage is also available. In addition to benefiting from PHW's broad range of insurance options, Livonia residents can expect personalized attention from "hometown" agents.

Under the impressive motto "Beginning Our Second Century of Service," Proctor Homer Warren is carrying on an impressive business history. In 1884 a firm known as Homer Warren & Company was founded. The independent firm of Proctor and Company came into existence 50 years later, during the 1930s. Both companies grew steadily, representing clients in buying, selling, managing, and insuring property.

In 1960 Proctor and Company acquired Homer Warren & Company, and in 1968 the two firms merged to become Proctor Homer Warren. The company built and moved into its modern atrium office building in Troy in 1975 and opened the Livonia agency in 1988. In addition to personal and commercial insurance, the firm insures banks and savings institutions.

Proctor Homer Warren, Inc., has assembled an extensive and impressive array of large corporate and business clients in southeastern Michigan over the years. Yet the company takes equal pride in the thousands of individual residents and business owners who are insured through PHW agents. Beginning its second century, PHW's commitment remains the same: to serve each client in the best possible way.

Proctor Homer Warren's headquarters in Troy.

HARRY J. WILL FUNERAL HOMES

Following the creed, "Professional people dedicated to personal attention," members of the Will family have been serving other families in the community for more than 50 years. The Harry J. Will Funeral Homes in Livonia and Redford reflect this philosophy. In beautiful, serene surroundings with a warm, caring atmosphere, the licensed and well-trained staff provide personal service for each funeral.

"Many families come back because they feel that services and arrangements were handled well," according to James Will, who has headed the firm since 1976. "Whether only a few people or 500 people attend, we try to make each service a fitting tribute to a unique life, and no effort is spared to meet each family's needs. Perhaps that is why we conduct the largest number of funerals in the area," Will adds.

The story behind the tradition goes back to the Depression years, when Harry J. Will did not have the money to study medicine, and he instead entered a two-year apprenticeship with a funeral director—Saturday night off, no pay, and free room and board. Eventually he received his license and worked as an independent funeral director; then he had the chance to purchase an established funeral home at Livernois and Michigan in Detroit.

As the population expanded to the west and north, Harry Will decided to expand with it, and he founded a business that his sons could enter as well. He bought land in Redford Township, and in 1962 one of the largest facilities designed especially for funeral services opened its doors at 25450 Plymouth Road.

By 1971 Will's oldest son, James, had entered the business, graduated from Wayne State University, and earned his license. Will's youngest son, Robert, was on his way to doing the same. The time was right to build a similar facility on land that Will bought at 37000 Six Mile Road near Newburgh. When this beautiful funeral home opened in 1974, it stood beyond the western edge of Livonia at that time.

The building in Livonia won an award for architectural design and landscaping. Inside, a two-story waterfall flows into a pond surrounded by flowering plants. Seven chapels plus other lounges and offices are furnished in soft pastel colors, creating a comfortable, serene atmosphere—a hallmark of the Will Funeral Homes.

The firm's founder, Harry J. Will, took an active role in the business until 1988. His son James became president in 1976, and his other son Robert now serves as vice president.

In the spirit of professionalism, the Harry J. Will Funeral Homes pioneered the practice of individually pricing items long before this was required by law. The firm also led in developing pre-need funeral arrangements, including no-payment and prepayment options. According to Robert Will, "Many people preplan their funerals to ensure that their wishes will be fulfilled and to make things easier for surviving family members."

Harry J. Will Funeral Homes is one of only 130 U.S. firms in the field to be invited to join both the International Order of the Golden Rule and the National Selected Morticians Association. As a public service experienced staff members frequently act as guest speakers to community groups.

Robert Will, vice president (left), and James Will, president.

MICHIGAN NATIONAL BANK

Michigan National Bank shares a solid and prosperous history with the City of Livonia. In 1953 five local business and professional leaders actualized their dream of establishing a state-chartered bank in the newly incorporated city, and the Bank of Livonia moved into its quarters across from the City Hall. Today, after nearly four decades in Livonia, the bank continues to help the individuals, corporations, and governments that once helped the bank to grow.

Through the 1960s and 1970s the bank worked to provide the region with a major financial hub as it expanded along with the community. When Michigan National Bank purchased a significant amount of the bank's stock in 1964, the institution was able to convert from a state to a national charter, and gained access to the latest in capital and management expertise.

Acquiring approximately $100 million in assets by 1972, the Bank of Livonia

became a full subsidiary of the Michigan National Corporation and was rechristened the Michigan National Bank-West Metro to reflect its increased financial prominence in the metropolitan area. In 1987 the corporation consolidated its operations, and local branches dropped the "West Metro" tag.

Today, with assets of over $11.6 billion, the Farmington Hills-based Michigan National Corporation has established 200 branches throughout the state, with nine in Livonia alone. A pioneer in branch banking since 1941, MNB introduced such innovations as the nation's first drive-up teller window in 1948, the state's first computerized banking operations center in 1959, and the largest automated teller machine network in Michigan today.

As a vital and thriving component of

the Michigan National Bank, the Livonia branches constantly strive to make banking services more convenient for customers and to expand the opportunities for financial partnership within the community. But first and foremost, Michigan National Bank wants to maintain its reputation as the bank that grew up with Livonia.

Michigan National Bank's new Livonia branch office at 33300 Five Mile Road opened in September 1989.

DEMERS ELECTRIC CO.

Alphonse J. Demers is the "man behind the lights" that shine in many of Detroit's and Livonia's public places. Demers, owner and president of Demers Electric Company since 1968, had charge of all electrical work for shows in Detroit's Cobo Hall between 1982 and 1987—a job that required hiring and supervising 120 men.

Demers was also responsible for electrical work on the Livonia Court House, Ford Field, the athletic fields at Churchill and Stevenson high schools, and the Walbridge Building at 6 Mile and Farmington roads, to name just a few of the company's better-known projects in Livonia.

The Canadian-born Demers came to Michigan in 1952, found work as an electrician, and decided to stay. Demers bought a house in Livonia in 1965 and at first worked for other local contractors.

In 1968, however, Demers started his own company out of an office in his

home. In 1970 Demers bought a building at 31715 8 Mile Road, where the company has its offices today.

Over the years Demers Electric Co. built up a solid reputation for doing high-quality electrical work for schools, office buildings, businesses, and industries. Architectural and engineering firms often request that Demers' company do the electrical work for their projects.

Demers is a long-time member of the chamber of commerce, a member of the Electrical Workers' Union Local 58, and was active in the National Independent Contractors Association and the Thomas Edison Club.

In recent years Demers' wife, Marie (vice president of the company) has become more active in the business as her husband has had to cut down his work. The Demers' son, Philippe, a business graduate of the University of Detroit, is now helping to carry on the company that has stood for honest workmanship since 1968.

Alphonse J. Demers, president of Demers Electric Co.

R.G. & G.R. HARRIS FUNERAL HOMES

Four generations of family ownership have created the R.G. & G.R. Harris Funeral Homes' tradition of caring for people in their time of need. The firm's growth and high standing in the community reflects the dedication of Harris family members over more than eight decades.

The company began in 1910, when 18-year-old Bob (R.G.) Harris returned from his apprenticeship in Sault Ste. Marie, Canada, and hung a sign on the front porch of the family home in Detroit. He became sole owner and the principal employee of the Robert G. Harris Undertaking Company. His father, George (G.R.), then worked as credit manager of the *Detroit Free Press,* but helped his son with the business during those first years.

In 1914 father and son formed a partnership—the R.G. & G.R. Harris Funeral Home—and moved the business to the old Haste Mansion on Trumbull Avenue in Detroit. The next 15 years saw the retirement of G.R.; R.G.'s year-long bout with a life-threatening infection, during which his father ran the company; and R.G.'s wife Flora getting a license and actively taking part in the business.

In 1930 the Harris Funeral Home started a very successful price advertis-

The attractive Harris Funeral Home at 15451 Farmington Road in Livonia has been extensively expanded and redecorated since the Harris family acquired it in 1964.

ing program. About the same time the landlady raised the rent on the Trumbull house, and the Harris Funeral Home moved to Cass Avenue. By 1941 the family had opened its first branch on Harper Avenue. The two homes soon built up a volume of about 800 services each year.

Detroit's population was shifting westward, and in 1964 the Harris company bought the Livonia Funeral Home on Farmington near Five Mile Road from Herbert and Millicent Harbin. They renamed it and soon added a chapel,

made extensive renovations, and acquired an additional parking lot. In 1970 the Harris family bought a funeral home in Garden City, on Ford Road near Merriman.

R.G. Harris died in 1966 at the age of 74. His son, Tom, and his son-in-law, Clarence Rost, carried on the business until their retirements. Clarence's son, Tom Rost, is now the fourth generation carrying on the family tradition. He is ably assisted by manager Mark Sayles and a carefully selected, experienced staff of more than 30 people who share responsibilities in the four Harris Funeral Homes.

The attractive funeral home on Farmington Road in Livonia is designed to put people at ease. There are two large chapels, smoking and nonsmoking lounges, a separate children's room, coffee room, and various offices in the tastefully decorated interior. The Harris Funeral Homes now offer a choice of selecting caskets and flowers by viewing slides, which many family members prefer.

"We want to go beyond the funeral service and offer more support for those who are trying to cope with the loss of someone near," Tom Rost says. The Harris' staff includes a grief therapist and psychologist, Dr. John Canine, and a community service representative, Helen Poppenger, whose services are available to grieving family members and friends. They act as co-leaders of an open support group and also speak to many educational, religious, and community groups on topics ranging from preplanning funeral arrangements to maximum living.

Some of the experienced, caring people at the Harris Funeral Homes: (back left to right) Lawrence Frohreip, manager; Roslyn C. Turner, secretary; Mark J. Sayles, manager; and Dr. John Canine, grief therapist; (front left to right) Tom Rost, president, James R. Rea, manager; David Sosnowski, funeral director; and James Berry, funeral director.

THE FELICIAN SISTERS OF LIVONIA

The distinctive provincial house of the Felician Sisters is the focal point of several institutions on their 320-acre property in Livonia. Through their ministry in education, health care, social services, and pastoral work, the Felician Sisters have been a significant influence in Michigan. Certainly Livonia would not be the same if they had not founded Madonna College, St. Mary Hospital, and Ladywood High School.

More than a century ago the Felician order in Poland sent five sisters to staff a school in Wisconsin. Transferring to Detroit in 1882, they gradually acquired land in Livonia and moved into the newly built provincial house in 1936. Today the Felician Sisters have provinces on four continents, with seven in the United States. Livonia is the headquarters of the oldest U.S. province.

A wing was added to the provincial house in 1950 for Madonna College before a separate campus was established. A beautiful chapel, begun in the Depression era, was finally completed in 1961. Three years later an infirmary was built, and in 1976 the Montessori Center of Our Lady was started. In September 1985 the Felicians established Angela Hospice to care for the terminally ill.

Over the years St. Mary Hospital, Madonna College, and Ladywood High School have increased their size through extensive construction in order to expand services for a growing clientele.

Today the Felician Sisters of Livonia have approximately 350 members, although only 150 currently live in the provincial house as others carry out their ministry in Michigan, Ohio, and Indiana.

MADONNA COLLEGE
Founded by the Felician Sisters in 1947, Madonna College has grown to an enrollment of more than 4,000 men and women of diverse ages, races, nationalities, and backgrounds. Madonna College's growth can be attributed to its quality programs, flexible scheduling options, affordable tuition, and accessible location. Students may earn associate and bachelor's degrees in more than 50 fields, including teacher education, business, nursing, science, and sign language studies. The college also awards a master of science in administration (MSA) degree with a specialty in business or educational leadership and a master of science degree in nursing (MSN). A dual degree master's program in nursing and business is also offered.

Today Madonna College continues its mission of fostering Christian humanistic values, intellectual inquiry, and service to others, and it successfully combines liberal arts with career preparation.

International in scope, Madonna has students studying abroad, a requirement of the International Studies program. The graduate program is offered in Taiwan, and Japanese studies was recently initiated as a minor field of concentration.

ST. MARY HOSPITAL
St. Mary Hospital is a full-service, 304-bed community hospital sponsored by the Felician Sisters. A landmark in Livonia and neighboring areas, St. Mary Hospital has served the community with the same spirit of Christian dedication since it opened in 1959.

St. Mary's highly skilled staff provides services in medical/surgical care, intensive/cardiac care, maternity, oncology, radiation therapy, mental health, chemical dependency, rehabilitation, and 24-hour emergency care.

Continuous hospital expansion programs have provided the community with state-of-the-art facilities and equipment. The St. Mary Hospital Pavilion offers convenient outpatient, diagnostic,

ABOVE, LEFT TO RIGHT:

The Felician Sisters' provincial house.

Madonna College's library.

St. Mary Hospital, with the new outpatient pavilion and the Marian Professional Building.

Ladywood High School.

and emergency services, while the Marian Professional Building houses physician offices and support services. Three satellite health care centers provide family-centered care close to home.

St. Mary Hospital is located at Five Mile Road and Levan in west central Livonia.

LADYWOOD HIGH SCHOOL
Ladywood, a fully accredited, college preparatory, private Catholic high school for girls, serves not only Livonia but all of western Wayne County. Founded in 1950 by the Felician Sisters of Livonia, it has grown and developed under dedicated administrators and certified teachers.

The philosophy of Ladywood aims to educate the whole person: spiritually, morally, intellectually, physically, and socially. It is committed to excellence, viewing each student as a unique individual, thereby providing not only basic high school courses but also a strong program of accelerated, honors, and advanced placement courses which help 98 percent of its graduates to go on to complete college. The students receive many honors and scholarships. The school promotes academic excellence, vibrant leadership, committed service, gracious personality, and strong character through an extensive sports program and clubs, and mainly through an active religious program of service to others.

BAYWOOD CLINIC, P.C.

One of the community's largest independent clinics, Baywood Clinic, P.C., provides mental health services for children, teenagers, and adults. In addition to its convenient location on Farmington Road, extended hours, and flexible fees, Baywood has more than a dozen highly qualified staff available to treat personal, family, marital, vocational, educational, and substance abuse problems.

Founded in 1973, Baywood is one of only a few outpatient psychiatric clinics close to Livonia to be approved by Blue Cross. The center is also licensed by the State of Michigan to provide substance abuse treatment programs.

With a staff of three M.D. board-certified psychiatrists, two licensed clinical psychologists, and eight certified clinical social workers, Baywood uses

The Baywood Clinic, P.C., has a professional staff of three board-certified psychiatrists, two Ph.D. clinical psychologists, and eight clinical social workers.

an interdisciplinary approach to treat individual and family problems. Among other things, this takes into account the psychological profile of the individual, the family structure, and other social and work-related factors. Medication is available if indicated.

Outpatient services at Baywood Clinic include evaluation and therapy in many areas: depression, anxiety, phobias, marital and divorce problems, adolescent problems, disability and legal assessments, eating disorders, and drug and alcohol abuse. Inpatient is available through referral to St. Mary Hospital and other area hospitals.

Psychological testing and evaluation can be made in several areas: intelligence, personality, career planning, substance abuse, preemployment screening, and workers' compensation. Baywood also provides training programs for private and public employers on topics ranging from stress to conflict resolution.

Baywood Clinic accepts referrals from all sources and also accepts all

major insurances. Guided by suggestions from its community advisory board, Baywood staff members present a series of free lectures on a broad range of mental health issues and are often invited to give talks and workshops to community groups.

Baywood Clinic's staff members are noted for their professional training and clinical experience. Dr. K.C.R. Nair, founder and head of the clinic, jointly owns and operates the facility with two other Michigan-trained doctors, also U.S. board-certified psychiatrists: Dr. Luis Pomodoro and Dr. Suhasini Mistry. Clinical staff members are specialists in particular areas, such as family counseling, eating disorders, and other fields.

The clinic plans to begin a weight-control program in 1991. Future plans include a lithium outpatient clinic and light therapy for sufferers from Seasonal Affective Disorders. Baywood Clinic's future seems to be solidly based on a broad range of treatment programs and an exceptionally well-qualified staff of specialists.

ASSOCIATED GROUP UNDERWRITERS, INC.

S ince we started in 1970, we've emphasized 'hometown service' to meet people's needs for house, auto, and RV insurance at competitive rates," says Paul Y. Kadish, president of Associated Group Underwriters, "and we've grown to be one of the largest independent agencies in the area." AGU represents another of Livonia's successful family-owned businesses, where customers can call or come in and get personal attention.

Today the agency also plays a key role in large self-insurance programs for Michigan community colleges and municipalities. Kadish serves as a risk manager for the Michigan Municipal Risk Management Authority (MMRMA), with responsibility for Livonia. The MMRMA was established in response to the increasing legal claims and lawsuits, rising insurance premiums, and decreasing coverage that local government agencies began to face in the past decade. The MMRMA now self-insures many cities and counties in the state and provides broad coverage at reasonable premiums.

Kadish also serves as risk manager for the Michigan Community College Risk Management Authority (MCCRMA), which self-insures 18 of the 29 community colleges in the state. As head of AGU, Kadish and his son, Ross, have sole responsibility for all participating Michigan community colleges, including Schoolcraft College in Livonia and Oakland Community College.

AGU remains primarily a family-oriented agency, however, in terms of its clients and its owners. Ross Kadish, who now serves as the firm's vice president, is a Chartered Property Casualty Underwriter and has qualified as an Associate of Risk Management. Debra Woods, Kadish's daughter, has worked in the family firm for more than 10 years, dividing her time between accounting and the customer service responsibilities. David Kadish, a recent graduate of Wayne State University, worked

The AGU team

part time in the agency for several years and now supervises AGU's branch offices.

In 1988 the agency moved its Livonia office from Wonderland Mall to the former Bentley house at 28095 Five Mile Road. AGU also has branch offices in Lincoln Park and Detroit.

Associated Group Underwriters has been serving Livonia residents since 1971, and its steady growth is largely

The Livonia office of AGU is located in the former Bentley house at 28095 Five Mile Road.

due to customer referrals as well as sales initiative. In the future, Associated Group Underwriters will further expand its writings of employee benefit programs.

"Until now, self-insurance was only feasible for large organizations. But we are learning more about how small businesses can group together to increase their insurance and employee benefit coverage at lower cost," Kadish says. "It's an exciting area that will develop in the years ahead."

SCHOOLCRAFT COLLEGE

Schoolcraft College recognizes that its mission as a public, tax-supported community college extends beyond the classroom and into jobs, businesses, community enrichment,

Schoolcraft College's unique belltower is a community landmark.

and personal development.

The college was founded in 1961 and more than 440,000 students have taken advantage of Schoolcraft College's wide-ranging curriculum and its commitment to meeting the educational needs of the community. "We have been successful in terms of job placement, transfers to four-year institutions, financial stability, and concern for our employees," says president Richard W. McDowell, "and we're doing our best to ensure that Schoolcraft College remains a vital community resource."

Schoolcraft College's tree-lined campus offers a pleasant learning environment. It emphasizes flexible programs, high-quality teaching, and close personal contact between students and professors. The college caters to a diverse population that includes recent high school graduates, mature students returning to improve their educational qualifications or to embark on a new career, and employ-

ees upgrading their professional skills.

Schoolcraft College's career programs provide students with specific job-related skills, while transfer programs prepare others to go on to a four-year college. Continuing Education Services offers more than 250 personal development classes plus professional development classes for law enforcement officers, real estate agents, chefs, and nurses.

More than $190 million in government contracts have been secured by area businesses and industries with the help of Schoolcraft's Business Development Center, which also works closely with local employers to provide customized training. Another outstanding area of the college is the culinary training program, recognized as one of the best in the nation. Finally, the community takes part in the many lectures, plays, and concerts offered on the Schoolcraft College campus during the year.

Photo by Bill Bachmann/Stills

BIBLIOGRAPHY

1: WELCOME TO THE FUTURE

Agenda magazine. Chrysler Corporation, July 1989.

Crain's Detroit Business. July 17, 1989.

Dunbar, Willis. *Michigan: A History of the Wolverine State.* Revised by George S. May, 1988.

Livonia Observer: April 3, 1986; May 12, 1988; November 3, 1988; and October 23, 1989.

Paris, Dominic P. *Footpaths to Freeways: The Story of Livonia.* 1975.

Romig, Walter. *Michigan Place Names.* 1988.

2: GREAT LIVONIA PEOPLE

Livonia Chamber of Commerce. *Facts on Livonia, 1988.*

_____. *Livonia Business and Community Directory, 1989.*

Livonia Observer: June 26, 1989; and September 28, 1989.

3: GREAT LIVONIA PLACES

Greenmead Tour Guide

Heart Fund Report, 1989.

The Koran

Livonia Chamber of Commerce. *Facts on Livonia, 1988.*

_____. *Livonia Business and Community Directory, 1989.*

Radway, Raymond F. *The Wayne, Plymouth and Northville Interurban.*

4: THE SPORTING LIFE

City of Livonia. Land Use Survey. May 1989.

City of Livonia, Department of Community Resources. *A Guide to Livonia City Services.* 1989.

City of Livonia, Department of Parks and Recreation. Annual Report, 1989.

_____. Program Bulletins, 1990.

Detroit Free Press. May 1, 1983.

Livonia Chamber of Commerce Community Calendar, 1990.

5: THE INFRASTRUCTURE

City of Livonia. Land Use Survey. May 1989.

City of Livonia, Department of Community Resources. *A Guide to Livonia City Services.* 1989.

Livonia Chamber of Commerce. Directory. 1989.

_____. *Facts on Livonia.* August 1988.

_____. Program Guide. 1990.

Livonia Observer, August 8, 1988.

Madonna College Media Kit, 1989.

Metropolitan Detroit Magazine. Livonia: Developing a Model City. July 1986.

Schoolcraft College Guide, 1989.

6: A CLIMATE FOR CULTURE

Hunt, Don and Mary. *Hunts' Guide to Southeast Michigan.* Midwestern Guides, 1990.

Livonia Chamber of Commerce. Annual guide, 1990.

Livonia Observer: May 14, 1990, and July 4, 1988.

Livonia Symphony Orchestra. Event guide, 1989-1990.

Monthly Detroit Magazine, March, 1990.

PATRONS

The following individuals, companies, and organizations have made a valuable commitment to the quality of this publication. Windsor Publications and the Livonia Chamber of Commerce gratefully acknowledge their participation in *Livonia: A Rich Past, A Golden Future.*

Argent Limited*
Associated Group Underwriters, Inc.*
Baywood Clinic, P.C.*
Charisma Salons*
Contractors Steel Company*
Corvo Iron Works, Inc.*
Demers Electric Co.*
Detroit Ball Bearing*
Embest, Inc., A Division of Country Fresh*
The Felician Sisters of Livonia*
Foodland Distributors*
General Motors—5 Divisions*
R.G. & G.R. Harris Funeral Homes*
Holiday Inn-Livonia*
Hughes Electronics Products Corp.*
Hygrade Food Products Corporation*
Kamp-DiComo Associates*

A.R. Kramer Company*
Laurel Park Place*
N. Leone & Sons, Inc.*
Livonia Mall*
LTV Missiles and Electronics Group*
Maurer-Shumaker, Inc.*
Michigan National Bank*
Parsons & Bouwkamp*
Proctor Homer Warren, Inc.*
Professional Food-Service Management, Inc.*
Schoolcraft College*
Schostak Brothers & Co., Inc.*
Stevens Design Service*
Technicolor Videocassette of Michigan*
United Parcel Service, Inc.
Harry J. Will Funeral Homes*
Wonderland Mall*

*Participants in Part Two, "Livonia's Enterprises." The stories of these companies and organizations appear in chapters 7 through 9, beginning on page 88.

INDEX